The Twenty Year Itch

Confessions of a Corporate Warrior

Amy Berger

Amy Berger

Illustrated by Elena Facciola

Motivational Magic Press

You can reach Amy at:
www.amyberger.com
aberger@home.com

Cover design by Scott Amaya, Amaya Design
Textual assistance by N.G. Meriwether
Art direction by John Berger

Motivational Magic Press
5604 Antone Road
Fremont, CA 94538
(510) 623-0787

Library of Congress Catalog Card Number: 99-90023
ISBN: 0-9665915-0-X

Printed in the United States of America by Bookmasters, Inc., P.O. Box 2139, Mansfield, Ohio 44905. 800-537-6727

January 1999

Dedicated to Susan J. Sparrow, my writing coach, John Berger, my husband, and God. Not necessarily in that order.

And to all my fellow corporate warriors out there—past, present and future.

Table of Contents

Introduction

I was tired of being unemployed. Actually, I was *exhausted.* Between sending out several resumes per day, networking—otherwise known as begging for job leads from total strangers—and weekly primal scream sessions with my therapist, the lack-of-work novelty was definitely wearing thin.

Actually, I was doing a lot of temp work during those days and preferred to call myself *'under-employed'* when asked what I did for a living. "Unemployed" has such a negative connotation. Every time I tried saying it the word stuck in my throat like bad peanut butter and images of being the world's youngest bag lady appeared, uninvited, in my head.

Non-work became a way of life for me. One day I decided that I could simply live the rest of my days in my cuddly teal bathrobe and throw away my contact lenses. That was the day I began to really worry—about myself. On the other hand, think of how much money I'd save on clothes!

One day I decided to get brave, go to a local cafe with the Classifieds, and treat myself to a glass of herbal iced tea. I am not much of a coffee drinker—bad for my PMS and *not* required for stimulation. My husband often reminds me that any caffeine intake on my part would likely result in turning me into Tornado Woman and be harmful to objects and people in my path.

Anyway, back to the cafe.

Settled in one of those gray steel, chic-looking but highly uncomfortable cafe chairs, I tried to relax and read the newspaper as planned. There were several other people in the place. *Were they the "U" word too, or just independently wealthy?* I wondered as I sipped my Rose Hips Splash and munched on a peanut butter cookie.

I felt like a newly released former resident of San Quentin as I looked around in amazement. *You mean not everyone in the world between 18 and 70 is a Corporate Slave—or a Corporate Slave wannabe—like me?! Where have I been all this time?! The world has changed and I'm the last to know!!*

Then I became nostalgic and memories of being employed flooded in. I remembered the times I used to take the morning off for a doctor's appointment. Those hours of freedom were precious. Now I had so much darn freedom I didn't know what to do with it. Be careful what you ask for, right?

As if I wasn't depressed enough, a homeless-looking guy sitting at the table next to mine suddenly introduced himself as Richard, hand outstretched. *Should I run? Start screaming for help? I finally get up the nerve to PUT ON CLOTHES AND LEAVE THE HOUSE and this happens! Oh God, why me?!*

In a moment of delirium I decided to trust this man and offered my hand to shake. One thing I had learned over the past three decades was---if you act confident you *are* confident. Otherwise known as 'fake it till you make it."

I began to ask this Richard person some questions. I soon learned that he was far from the serial killer he may have resembled. In fact, Richard had worked at AT&T as a technician, was married to a woman who was a seamstress and had two grown children. He had *just* been laid off from a blue-collar job at that corporate monolith—after THIRTY years.

No wonder he looked homeless—the poor guy was in a state of shock.

Feeling pretty guilty about my false assumptions about Richard, I decided it was time to put on my Counselor Amy cap and do something useful. If I couldn't seem to get myself a job then at least I could help someone else find a way to support himself. As we continued to talk, I offered him some job hunting suggestions. I even asked him to send me his resume so I could keep an eye out for a potential position for him. I believe what comes around goes around and I needed something, *anything* to come around quick!

We were mirrors of each other since I was still mourning the loss of my job at a large San Francisco Bay area corporation. But let me tell you, the reflection wasn't pretty. Sitting there with him, I thought we could be a great poster couple for the Salvation Army Vocational Training program.

As we refugees from the corporate war zone continued to chat, I learned that Richard loved to draw and had been doing so for most of his life. On the side, of course. (God forbid he should get paid for something he loves to do.) I guess I was pretty bitter at this point in my journey down the Brown Brick Road Toward Poverty.

He showed me some examples of his sketches and described himself to me as " A good wine before its time." In his heart he knew he was special but, after thirty years working in a telephone plant, he found it easier to keep that artist-self tucked away. I didn't know whether to cry or punch out the next man or woman in a charcoal gray suit who crossed my path.

I was reading the Marsha Sinetar book *Do What You Love and the Money Will Follow* during those days and had begun to believe that with hard work and passion, we humans *could* get paid for doing stuff we liked and found easy.

"Don't give up the ship!" I yelled.

Well, not in so many words. But I sure felt like a cast member of *Mutiny on the Bounty* that day. Rebelling against that monster called Unemployment. *Didn't Richard see that people like he and I were God's children? Poor, depressed and slightly neurotic but, definitely talented?*

I began to despair until I got a brilliant thought.

I told Richard I wanted to 'commission' a drawing from him. To my delight, my fellow misfit agreed to do the drawing right then and there. I don't know why I was so surprised at his reply. Like either of us had anything better to do that day?

Maybe this guy was psychic because the next thing I knew he had pulled out a piece of plain white 8" by 11" paper from his worn satchel and begun to draw. By this time my long-haired friend and I were seated at the same table and we were practically planning our honeymoon.

Within minutes he had drawn a beautiful sketch of a rose, artistically wrote "To Amy" in the lower right hand corner of the page, dated and signed it. We walked together over to the nearby copy shop where I paid for the drawing to be copied on mauve parchment paper. That was all the commission Richard wanted—such a deal!

My afternoon with Richard inspired me, six years later, to write this book about surviving the ups and downs of Corporate

America. Although I *was* fully employed when I wrote it, I realized that someday I might not be. Every day I hear on the radio about the hundreds—no, thousands—of people who get laid off from their jobs. One of them could again be me.

Now, I'm no flaming liberal or anything—in fact to the shock of some ex-hippie friends I've just registered Republican—but I understand business economics quite well. The thing is, even if you can see why downsizing makes sense for an organization's bottom line, it still *hurts* when it happens to you.

When your boss takes you into that little conference room in the back of the office and closes the door with a weird expression on her face.

It hurts.

When she starts out the conversation by saying, "Most people like to spend the rest of the day walking on the beach when something like this happens…" and you feel like you just swallowed a boulder from the film *The Flintstones*….

It hurts.

When she's holding a funny looking envelope in her hand that kind of looks like a check could fit in it, but you *know* it's not payday. And you just put a down payment on a new minivan…..

It hurts.

And when, even before she opens her guilt-ridden mouth to tell you you've been canned for no reason and you want to hit the floor writhing like a person who's just had their jacket set on fire, screaming—*No! No! Please don't say it! Take my dog! Take my pension plan! Take my spouse! Take anything but please don't take my job!*— it really hurts.

So, for all of us Corporate Warriors, here are some true confessions, and perhaps a little inspiration, from one who's been there.

Chapter 1
Getting There: On the Lethal World of Commuting

It was another misty morning in the San Francisco Bay Area. I prepared for battle:

Vehicle inspection. (I wiped down the windows)

Check.

Rations. (Placed my sack lunch on the seat)

Check.

Protective gear. (Strapped on my seat belt)

Check.

Equipment test. (Turned on my radio)

Check.

I was ready for action.

I turned on the ignition, backed slowly out of my driveway and proceeded cautiously down my suburban street. My primary challenge was to NOT hit too many moving objects. As I crept along at six miles per hour, I negotiated my way through schoolkids on skateboards, large garbage bins being wheeled into garages by anal retentive homeowners and of course, other groggy drivers.

My daily commute had begun.

Life in the fast lane isn't all it's cracked up to be. But then, how would I know? It's rare that I reach 40 MPH during *my* daily trek to the office. Believe it or not, the pace of my journey to work is *nothing* compared to the trauma I endure just trying to get on the darn freeway.

Many mornings as I approach the highway on-ramp I pray *please God, let there be movement. I know 50 miles per hour might be asking too much, but how about 30?*

It gets worse.

From the top of the overpass, hands wringing and heart palpitating, I force myself to look down on an awful scene below: bumper to bumper, chrome to chrome, snails! I turn my eyes heavenward. *This is no way to start the day.* And when I'm on the actual freeway I find myself wondering *Why do they call it a FREEway? Free from what?*

Philosophy 101 was not favorite subject in high school.

Now that I've reached the All Powerful Concrete Path to Nowhere, I need to get into the line of traffic, right? Have you ever tried to merge into a line of cars, barely two feet from each other, that are inching along at a mere 5 miles per hour? It's like trying to insert a piece of dental floss between two carefully wedged teeth---in the back of your mouth. It ain't easy.

As I politely inch my way up to what I think might be part of an open space that maybe a car could fit into, a small muscle in the middle of my forehead starts throbbing and I begin to hyperventilate.

What if no one lets me in? What if I'm stuck here all day with my left-turn signal on? What if I'm still here 300 years from now with my fists wedged onto the steering wheel like a barnacle on the side of a sunken barge in the middle of the Black Sea?

As the perspiration cascades down my face like Niagara Falls, taking my mascara with it, I notice that a car has actually stopped.

Did I forget to put in my contact lenses? Am I hallucinating from the sleeping pill I took last night when my husband began to snore so loudly the wallpaper in the master bathroom started peeling?

No. It is not a mirage of any sort. To my astonishment, this is real. The driver is waving his hand, *inviting* me to enter the lane of traffic.

I can barely believe it.

I want to jump out of my car, run over to this perfect stranger, fling my body on top of his and scream *I love you!! I want to have your babies!! You actually let me into the lane---you must be an ANGEL!*

But I don't.

I simply take my place in line, give him a sugary smile like Shirley Jones in *Oklahoma*, and a hand signal that says "Thanks so much. You just saved my life. Have a good day."

Believe it or not, commuting also has its pleasures. The sights I behold while I plod along are better than what's on TV.

One day I had the pleasure of driving behind Aretha Franklin. Or at least she thought she was. This gal was booming it out for a full five minutes as she listened to one of her favorite tunes. Bouncing up and down, flailing her arms, gesticulating, smiling, laughing and of course SINGING. Too bad her windows were shut. I couldn't hear a darn thing. If I had, I could've joined her in a duet for the road.

On second thought, I'm no Bette Midler so maybe the other commuters were spared that morning.

"THE MORNING COMMUTE"

Then there are the other Freeway Flyers personalities:

- Passive-Aggressive Patty: the person who smiles sweetly at you while you ask her via a variety of hand gestures and silly facial expressions, if you may cut in line. Two seconds later she zooms ahead as you begin to edge over into her lane.

- Zombie Zelda: the person who does not even blink as she creeps along in traffic, eyes straight ahead, mesmerized by the bumpersticker on the car in front of her that says, "My Kid Beat Up Your Honor Student." Is she a human being, I wonder, or one of those fake-but-designed-to-look-real people you see at Disneyland?

- Salesmaniac Stu: the person who literally has a cellular telephone growing out of his right ear.

- You-Want-Me-to-*Drive*? Donald: the person who is primping in the mirror, gabbing with his friend, sending a fax or doing anything other than keeping his eyes on the road.

Other enjoyable sights I've experienced along the Mental Institution Highway (M.I.H.) have included: a man with his face painted part black, part silver; a large tattoo of a ship's anchor which was probably attached to an arm somewhere, a sports car with a convertible top that lifted 18 inches up via four small metal posts, a man with a green backpack, meandering his way down the side of the road. He probably abandoned his vehicle in search of a more efficient form of transportation—his feet.

And of course bumper stickers and license plate frames, like my favorites: *Quilt While You're Ahead* and *Honk If You Like Meatloaf.*

One day there were the Terminator Twins to liven things up. Two almost identical white cars, were driving side by side in their separate lanes. I was driving behind one of these white metal beasts, minding my own business.

As we three automobiles edged closer to the exit ramp, the two lanes merged. That's when White Car Number One and White Car Number Two began to fight.

At first it was subtle. One car tried to get ahead of the other by gently inching forward. The other car would have no part of it and matched the movement. It went like that for a while. Back and forth. Back and forth. As each car took its turn one-upping the other. Cordially, at first, then with downright violence.

Before I knew it, White Car Number One literally bumped White Car Number Two out of its way. But no one got out of the car to offer a telephone number so I figured something mean was up. Clearly someone was going to die by getting *dinged to death* before this fight was over.

I sat there in horror and fascination as the rivalry continued. It was like watching an intense game of bumper cars where all the cars were going the same direction and they were all the same color.

Honey, please pass the popcorn, I muttered under my breath.

After another 45 minutes—okay, it was only 10 seconds but it sure seemed like a long time—I noticed a long black pole with a little white flag slowly being pushed through the open sunroof of White Car Number Two. (The things people keep in their cars these days!) Somber music began to play from somewhere on the freeway and the woman in the car next to me began to weep. White Car Number Two had surrendered and was allowing White Car Number One to pass in front. Hallelujah! No blood was shed but, boy, was Joe's Body Shop at the next off-ramp going to be happy.

Now *that's* what I call a Drive-In movie.

How To Stay Sane in Rush Hour Traffic

- *Lower your standards.* Sure, you know a 12 mile freeway trip should only take around 20 minutes under normal conditions. Plan for abnormal conditions and you'll be happy when you pull into your destination at just under 55 minutes.

- *Make new friends.* Try smiling at the fellow zombie in the car next to you. You'll either get arrested for sexual harassment, allowed space in the next lane over—since that person has pulled away quickly to avoid further eye contact—OR you may even get a smile in return. Whichever way it goes it will perk up your nasty commute.

- *Do household chores.* Or at least think about them. Write down all the things you could be doing at home while you're piddling away your precious time locked in your car on the freeway. *Hmmm.* On second thought, maybe you should scratch that one.

- *Shave. Put on makeup. Do your hair.* The day you see someone doing all three will really be fun. Seriously, though...one morning my husband was appalled when I walked out of the house with a full set of pink curlers perched on my head. "What's the problem, Dear?" I retorted. "This is called morning efficiency!"

- *Sing. Dance. Write Letters to Loved Ones.* Allright, dancing could be a little tough. But singing and writing (via a portable microcassette recorder) are both quite doable. People will think you're a VIP, talking very seriously into an unrecognizable little black box.

- *Eat.* Breakfast-via-car-seat is an old American tradition. My buddy Ralph knew of a woman who learned to eat Chinese food while steering her car---with chopsticks, no less. Eating, that is, not driving.

Chapter 2: Better Homes and Cubicles: Thoughts on Office Decor in the Nineties

Aquariums with brightly colored fish. Basketball hoops suspended seven feet high. Dart boards. Teddy bears. Wind up gadgets. Gumby.

The toy section of Wal-Mart?

A chic new shop at the mall for recreational objects?

Heck no.

We're talking office decor in Corporate America. It's amazing what we middle managers and line-workers will go through to make our cubicles and offices feel like home.

I was on the Safety Committee for one firm several years ago. Our job was to inspect every office or cube in the building to look for irregular electronic plugs and other hazardous conditions. My first 'beat' was the Engineering Department.

For some reason, 99% of those guys and gals had life size murals of wilderness scenes taped behind their many layers of gray, black, white and cream-colored electronic equipment. While PC monitors buzzed with fuzzy lines of hardware specs or software code, majestic mountains, raging rivers and mellow meadows hung silently on the walls behind. After four or five cubes which boasted the same darn view of the outdoors, I felt like I was at a Zen Buddhist retreat. *Where's my meditation cushion and herbal tea?*

There were, of course, exceptions to this standard haute decor. Like the 4 by 5 foot headshot of some blonde-haired, blue eyed supermodel. *I'll bet she doesn't have three college degrees!* I silently fumed as I turned a light shade of green—with envy. *Why do some men still prefer blondes for their pin-up girls?*

And of course there was the Petrified Cake Museum. One of these computer nerds had a collection of six month old slices of birthday cake—of varying colors—perched atop a five-inch black plastic plate. A small sign which hung underneath cited an admission fee of $3.00. Not a bad deal for an afternoon's entertainment. There was also a suspension bridge created out of empty soda cans and paper clips. Our Engineering department was becoming more fun than Six Flags Over Who Knows Where!

I'll never forget the time I was suspended from my job for a week for trying out a little office decorating myself. I was working for a private, non-profit organization in a low-income section of Los Angeles. The funny thing about this community-service group was that our finances were geared more to keeping the Executive Director in a brand new Mercedes 250SL than on our clients or employee working conditions. Instead of moving to a larger building, as the organization grew, the powers that be just kept adding burnt-orange colored 6 foot by 14 foot partitions to create new offices.

My cube felt like 13 inches by 10 inches. And that was when I held my breath. After having nightmares of suffocating to death in my office, I decided to take matters into my own hands. I arrived early one morning and, after much huffing and puffing, pushed one Evil Orange wall back about 2 and a half feet. *Ah. That's better. Now I can breathe and actually think again---that is if my brain cells haven't already died from asphyxiation.*

A sweet but short victory that was, however. My boss got in the office an hour later and went utterly ballistic. He was furious that I hadn't asked the janitor to move the wall for me—according to office standards. He yelled for another ten minutes and proceeded to suspend me.

I was furious and humiliated. After all, I was *just* trying to help. So, what does an up-and-coming corporate professional do when something like this happens? Why, run home to Mommy and Daddy, of course! I went directly to my parents' backyard pool, worked on my tan and spent the rest of the afternoon with the Classifieds.

Speaking of office walls, I had one cubicle that was so substandard that one of the three walls periodically fell down, with a notable *thud* leaving a six and a half foot by five and a half foot gaping hole. Not that I, sitting at my desk, feeling like a Go-Go Dancer in an open cage, was a half-bad sight, mind you. The problem was that the worn and dirty beige burlap partition, lying prostrate on the floor, looked indeed tacky. Not to mention a bit of a distraction for my surrounding colleagues.

Come to think of it, that was the same company that had a leaky ceiling. At my 40th birthday party a dear friend of mine (who had also worked there) reminded me of the time I pointed out this building characteristic to a representative from OSHA, in front of one of the company VeePees. Oh well. *Someone* had to explain the yellow slickers and galoshes inside the building.

...COULD YOU HOLD FOR JUST A MOMENT, PLEASE?!

Before I neglect yet another fun office decor experience at that same firm, a technology research company, I must relay the story of the Victoria's Secret™ Christmas Tree. It was the holiday season and our floor wanted to decorate. After we brought in a traditional, five foot green pine tree, everyone was encouraged to contribute decorations. I was hoping that folks would actually *buy* things like green and red shiny balls and even an angel or two. Leave it to my colleagues to add things that were reminiscent of their area of interest. Before I could stop them, we had software diskettes, computer chips and assorted samples of medical equipment strewn across the tree. The articles included a half dozen white surgical head coverings which, viewed from a distance, resembled underwear. Well, so much for Norman Rockwell's Christmas!

Then there was Christmas season when I learned what being a stranger in a strange land is all about. There was a hall decorating contest held at our 400-person firm. Each department was asked to doll up the walls in their section of the building according to the winter holiday theme. I participated in our department's decorating committee and helped decide that candy cane stripes over white tissue paper would be our contest contribution.

Chanukah—the Jewish Festival of Lights that occurs around the time of Christmas— was never mentioned.

I helped buy the stuff for the department decorations and put the payment on my expense account.

Chanukah was never mentioned.

I helped tape 130 million sheets of 3 foot by 3 foot white tissue paper squares onto 2500 ugly brown office partitions.

Chanukah was never mentioned.

When we used 50 rolls of bright red crepe paper to create an interminable number of candy canes, Chanukah was never mentioned—but now I started to feel bad. I heard the voice of my Polish ancestors yelling (we Jews aren't taught to talk softly when expressing ourselves): "*Amela*...why aren't you speaking up?! We worked for thousands of years— (do you ever notice how Jews always say THOUSANDS of years when we refer to our struggles? Like hundreds aren't good enough?)— to get respect from the world. Don't hide! Get in there and take a stand!"

I decided that the very next day I would tiptoe out to the local drugstore and buy some sweet little Chanukah decoration to put in my cube. No muss, no fuss.

But somehow my colleagues beat me to it.

When I arrived at work the next morning I beheld a HUGE star of David— the "Jewish Star"— crafted lovingly from light blue tissue paper, taped to the front of my cubicle. Suddenly I could relate to my Eastern European brethren who had tattoos on their arms during WWII. I didn't know whether to laugh or cry, but I did neither. I did something better. I went to the cafeteria and bought a jelly donut.

Another important part of office decor is, of course, the HVAC. (No. This is not short for "Hey, There's a Vacant Cubicle!" Rather, it means Heating, Ventilation and Air Conditioning.

If some medical researcher ever ventured to do a study that compares the probability of catching a cold *indoors* in one's cubicle, with the same probability of catching a cold while wearing a T-shirt and shorts and playing Frisbee Golf in Antarctica, cube life would win hands down.

I swear there are little midgets up in the ceilings at America's offices, hired by CEOs to place fresh ice cubes in front of the air ducts every fifteen minutes. Even when the heat is supposed to be turned on, it is typically *freezing* in my office. I once had a colleague who often turned a lovely shade of periwinkle blue, because her cube was dysfunctionally wired. Our cubicles were so close I could hear her teeth chattering.

Speaking of temperature controlling devices, my new pint-sized yet very effective space heater came in particularly handy for office decoration one day. I ran out to the store to pick up something for the office and when I returned to my car it began to rain. Not mist. Not drizzle. But RAIN. Cats, dogs, iguanas, horses, whatever else you want to throw in. It was WET. Of course that was the day I was wearing my cute T-strap red shoes with lots of room for water to seep into them. When I returned to my cube my socks were *soaked.* Every time I took a step you could hear *squish, squish, squish* in the next town over!

Then I got a brilliant idea. *Why not use my brand new space heater to dry out my socks?! It will only take a few minutes and in the meantime I can still wear my shoes.*

So off came the socks and I secretly draped them across the top of the heater, which was humming away innocently in the corner of my cubicle. Then I proceeded on with my work day, forgetting about the dilemmas of my feet. About forty-five minutes later, when I returned to my cube I was surprised to find a group of colleagues. With silly smiles across their faces. *Oh God! Did they find the secret stash of gummy bears I keep in my top drawer? Or that picture of me in a teeny weenie bikini taken in Hawaii several months before? Or my list of affirmations that included, 'I will not beat my head against the wall no matter how bad it gets around here'?*

JULY
1998
Elena '98

Luckily I discovered that it was none of above. It was— my socks! They were so amused at seeing my laundry in my cubicle that they were ready to take a photo for the company newsletter. *Wasn't anyone else at the company ever in the Scouts?* Better that my socks were hung out to dry that day, than me.

Then there was the story of the rainbow piñata. Actually there were two. Stories, not piñatas. But we'll start with one.

I have a thing about rainbows. I love them. Refrigerator magnets, T-shirt designs, wall hangings, key chains. Even photographs of real ones. I can't get enough of them. One day I got it in my head that I had to have a piñata in the shape of a rainbow. So, every time I passed one of those Mexican grocery stores with the piñatas hanging out front, I'd crane my neck to get a closer look. Astronauts in bubble helmets; Alice in Wonderland lookalikes; Barney™ the Dinosaur, even a computer monitor. But no rainbows. After a while I confessed my desire to my husband and he, too, started looking for a rainbow-shaped piñata.

Six months later, driving home from an exciting lunch at KFC™, we saw it. Hanging there outside an out-of-the-way Mexican grocery store---a rainbow piñata!

"STOP THE CAR!! Turn around! There's my rainbow piñata!" I screamed, watching my husband's blonde, stick-straight hair stand up on end. Sure enough, he peeled a U-turn and stopped the car in front of the store. I ran out to embrace the brightly-colored-tissue-paper-covered-cardboard-upside-down-U like it was my long-lost lover.

It was a beautiful sight.

After being in our home for a few weeks, I decided to brighten up my office at work with this special item. I was so excited as I hung up that piece of art over my cube. Violet, blue, fuscia, orange, yellow—a rainbow was finally swinging gracefully over my head from nine to five. It was heaven.

Until comments from my colleagues started rolling in.

"Did you bring that in, Amy?"

"No. It's from the Tooth Fairy" I responded dryly.

"Is it filled with candy?"

"No. It's for decoration."

"When can we break it open?"

"Never. If you touch my piñata I'll break your neck."

The piece-de-resistance was the Vice President of Sales. Apparently he scoped it out one day, when I was absent, and told one of his cronies to have a word with me.

"Uh, Amy, about your piñata," stammered Regional Manager Robert.

"Yeah, Bob, isn't it great?"

"Yeah. Hmm. Of course. But you know, Frank says...."

"What DOES Frank say, Bob?" I clenched my fists, practically ruining my manicure.

"He, uh, thinks that maybe, it stands out too much, and, maybe it doesn't look right in the office, and...and…"

"And WHAT, Bob?" I stepped closer and barred my freshly scrubbed teeth—glad I had been to the dentist that morning.

"Uh…Uh... and that it looks like a toy store...and uh…uh..."

My index finger was poking his wimpy chest at this point. "Does he, now, Bob? You just tell Mister Frank that he can pass on by if my piñata bothers him—and—and…" The next thing I saw was the back of Bob's bald head as he tore off down the hall, Brooks Brothers shirt tails flapping behind him. "AND TELL FRANK TO SEE ME HIMSELF IF HE HAS A PROBLEM WITH MY OFFICE DECOR!!!"

No one messes with my rainbow piñata.

No one.

<u>How to Survive FCS—Frozen Cube Syndrome</u>

- Cover up the vents with manila folders and Scotch tape. Even if this trick does not keep out the cold air, your workspace will look so tacky that management will get the hint.

- Plug in a cheap space heater and blow a circuit that takes down your computer and 5 others in your section of the building. Another attention getting device when the above is ineffective.

- Develop a physical ailment and take off three weeks on state disability. That will give you several good shopping days to stock up on winter wear.

- Learn to work in a parka, ski hat and wool gloves that you bought in Suggestion Number 3.

- Pray for a transfer to your company's Miami Beach office. Enough said.

Chapter 3:
Dress and Regress: Reflections on Office Attire

The president just finished presenting the company numbers at our All Personnel Meeting. You know---revenues, unit shipments and the like. We sat there in our removable plastic chairs, shifting like anxious kindergartners, eager to be dismissed. Then she asked it.

"Are there any questions at this point? I'm sure some of you have questions." *Darn*, I muttered to myself. *This boring business meeting is so long it's going* ***beyond*** *Here to Eternity.*

"Yeah. I have a question." Someone had actually raised their hand. "When will we get to wear shorts again?" Ahhhh. I was deeply touched by depth of my colleague's insightful question— so proud to be part of this inquisitive group!

That's Corporate America. We employees spend 45 interminable minutes on heavy corporate stuff like stock purchase price and revenue goals and all anyone *really* cares about is what to wear.

I'll never forget the image presented to me by my ex-husband of one of his Engineering Department colleagues. A woman who wore flowered shirts and plaid pants.

At the same time.

Mind you, Corporate America is a veritable fashion parade.

We mustn't forget the other colleague of a friend of a friend— woman who wore her hair in pigtails. No, she definitely wasn't under the age of ten. Come to think of it, she wasn't under the age of forty, either. Without even meeting her, this gal reminded me of a grown-up Pippi Longstocking. You know, that goofy-looking but cute little girl with red hair and freckles who lived in the children's section of your average 1960's bookstore? I guess she's still inspiring women of my generation how to dress.

Then there was the time I invited my parents to meet me for lunch. I was working in one of those fancy high-rise office buildings in West Los Angeles. The kind that looks like an impenetrable all-glass monolith from a Hollywood movie. You may have seen it in Arnold S's most recent sci-fi flick.

I dressed up especially for the occasion in my Early Eighties Career Woman costume. Navy blue suit, white blouse with bow at the neck, beige pantyhose and navy blue pumps. I looked maahvelous!

At least *I* thought so.

The first thing out of my mother's mouth when she saw me was "Nice ensemble—you look *just* like a stewardess!"

So much for dressing for success.

That incident was not half as appalling, however, as the afternoon I walked through half the building with my skirt split up the back! Of course it was the day I decided *not to* wear a slip as well as the day I decided to wear bright green panties. Thank God I was rescued by a friendly, female co-worker with a safety pin before I could really give the company something to talk about.

In my decades as Corporate Slave Number 2,236,896,999 I have observed several clothing styles and have participated in the endless Office Fashion Show. After many trials and tribulations that go along with being a fashion plate of the business scene, I now wear my pajamas to work. At least *some* people have accused me of that.

I was sitting in my cubicle one Wednesday morning, minding my own business, decked out in one of my California-Casual-But-Elegant-Sweatsuits. All of a sudden one of my colleagues stopped by to say hello on her way back to her cell. Uh… I mean cube.

She took one look at me and gave me a big frown.

Have you ever seen a highly educated, well- to-do career woman grimace? It isn't pretty.

"Gosh Amy, you get all decked out on Casual Fridays yet you wear your pajamas to work every *other* day of the week! I don't get it!" Apparently she had seen me in my corporate costume that one and only Friday when I had a meeting to attend.

Some people are so cranky.

That pajama comment came back to haunt me, though, like indigestion after a greasy pizza. Roughly one year and one company later I was making my way back from the copy machine in my waffle-cloth-baby-pink empire-waisted long dress. A typical work ensemble for me at this age and stage. I felt a little like a cross between Queen Guenevere, TinkerBell and a pink California Raisin™. After so many years of tight skirts, tight panty hose and uptight bosses I felt I earned the right to have naked legs again at work.

MR. HEADLY, WILL YOU EXPLAIN OUR CASUAL FRIDAY POLICY TO MS. JONES?
ELENA '98

As I passed the cube of a fellow female employee she called out, "Hey Amy, I love your dress. It looks so comfy it reminds me of my nightgown!"

There was that blasted sleepwear theme again. Just because I am lucky enough to live in California and work in the Silicon Valley where dress codes are, relaxed—uh—would you believe non-existent?—people get all fussy.

I am a firm believer in comfort before beauty. Especially in the workplace. If I can't breathe, I can't work. Plain and simple.

The other day at work I wore a brand new hot-pink *crinkly* (that's the technical term determined by the Fashion Institute of American Business Women's Attire) skirt to work. You know, the kind that is guaranteed to catch on fire with just the slightest help from a Boy Scout with two extra pick-up sticks? I was at my desk, sipping my morning addiction—chamomile tea—when I started to hyperventilate.

My breathing became shallower and shallower and I'm sure my face began to turn blue. (Not a bad color for me actually but it would have clashed that day.) Was I having an anxiety attack over the project I was working on? Did the air conditioning vent suddenly close, blocking the stream of air blowing through my cubicle? What was happening?!

I didn't know why, but all of the sudden I couldn't breathe! Then I realized it wasn't stress or a building malfunction. No. Something on my body was causing the problem.

Was it my new earrings? No. They were uncomfortable, but not enough to block my windpipe. Could it be my new shoes? Nope. I was wearing some old ones that day.

It was something around my waist. Something so tight that my cheeks started filling up with precious air and I began to feel like a balloon entry for Macy's Thanksgiving Day parade. In fact, MY ELASTIC WAISTBAND WAS SQUEEZING ME TO DEATH!!!

What to do, what to do? I feverishly wondered. Drive home to change clothes? I was feeling too lazy for that. Strip down to my slip and explain that it was the newest fashion trend—Underwear as Outerwear? Although my bra strap and/or slip are often in the public viewing arena —and not by choice— I wasn't ready for that one.

Ah Ha! I've got it! I squealed to myself in glee as the remedy for my predicament became crystal clear. *CUT THE SKIRT.* Yes. It would be a simple task really. I felt like Sherlock Holmes and Dr. Watson rolled into one, as I twisted my mustache and remained deep in thought.

"What, she's got a mustache?" you may ask. After dying, plucking and/or chemically obliterating those irksome hairs on my upper lip, I still can't get rid of the darn thing. In this case, it came in handy.

So, back to the skirt.

Just a quick snip to the waistband and I would be a liberated woman again. While I really liked the garment, it cost only $10 at JC Penney and could easily be replaced. I silently grabbed my weapon—a large, orange-plastic-handled pair of scissors— from my desk drawer and started planning my attack.

It may hurt. It may look silly. But the War Against Uncomfortable Clothing is ugly and the deed had to be done. Like a Japanese fighter pilot about to commit harikari I held the large shears up to my throbbing waistline and began to—WAIT! I quickly reminded myself that this act could look odd to the average passerby. I didn't want others to start rumors about me trying to bisect myself on company time with a locally available sharp instrument. If I was going to dismember myself at work then I wanted to start the rumors myself! Why let *them* get all the glory?

I decided to go to the Ladies' Room. It was a piece of cake. One snip here, the other there and one could hardly notice the change. With each small incision into the brightly colored cloth I felt like a balloon being deflated. No more pressure. No more pain.

Ahhhhhh. Life was good. In fact, the skirt ended up looking better with a softer waistband and I got a ton of compliments on my outfit that day.

Go figure.

How To Dress For Success or Comfort (Take Your Pick)

- Forget all the fashion tips your mother told you. She never had a 10-hour-a-day corporate job in the Nineties—what does *she* know?

- Spend very little money on clothes. Whatever you wear will get torn on the office furniture, nuked in the office microwave or tagged by every writing implement you own, so why waste the funds?

- Minimize accessories—they will likely be lost, stolen or eaten by the office shredder.

- Memorize and wear the company colors as much as possible—it could mean the difference between a promotion or a new job somewhere else.

- Always carry a change of clothes—what with hazardous materials like coffee, soda pop, ink, toner from the copy machine, candy and sweet rolls you never know when you'll need to make a quick change.

Chapter 4:
On Colleagues: People...Who Hate People.... Are the Luckiest People in the World

I was sitting at my desk, early one morning, innocently drinking my herbal tea when I first heard it. It was a distinct sound —a cross between a cackle, a choking sound and a voice that had just been altered by a little puff of helium going down the windpipe. As it persisted, the noise became increasingly irritating, kind of like fingernails scraping on a chalkboard. As I drew in a long deep breath to steady my nerves, I wondered *What in God's name is that awful noise?*

Then it came to me. The noise came from a human being and it was a laugh—though more like the kind of chuckle that they have in The House of Horrors at amusement parks—but nonetheless a laugh. And it was insipid. Insidious. All those 'I' words that mean EXTREMELY ANNOYING. Especially first thing in the morning.

As much as I wished I *was* at Six Flags, gliding down a fake mountain in a little wooden cart with the wind in my hair, I wasn't. I was back in my office being driven mad by a colleague who was yucking it up with another employee. Thus started another case of the Workaday Colleague Blues.

Let's face it, we can't love *everyone* we meet at work, and God forbid they should *all* love *us.* So, in order to survive, we must scope out the following personality types so we can plan our avoidance techniques:

- Those we must work with if we expect to receive a paycheck.
- Those we like to be around, but only between 9 and 5.
- Those we despise and steer clear of from DAY ONE.
- Those rare ones that could possibly be—dare I say it?—*friends.*

The savvy corporate employee easily detects the differences between these species and quickly goes about building her/his alliances. And speaking of the most important alliance one can have, bosses must be scoped out early (like after you've introduced yourself at the interview), and with finesse, in order for corporate survival to take place. I have run across these several boss-types in my years in Corporate America. Do any of these sound familiar?

HAAHAHAHA HAAHA HA HA HA HA
HA HA HA HA HA HA
HAAHAAHAHA
HA HHAHAAAHAHAHA

- Insecure Ian: the kind that yells rather than talk; leaps rather than looks; becomes more paranoid with each successive accomplishment you make and finally fires you because he's afraid that you'll take his job.
- Empire-Builder Ethel: a derivative of the above; usually feels so incompetent (mostly because she is) that she must surround herself with old cronies in order to create false job security.
- Sadistic Stephanie: hates herself and her life so she makes sure everyone else feels the same by setting up unrealistic job expectations.
- Masochistic Matthew: surrounds himself with vendors, superiors and subordinates that are obnoxious, arrogant or downright mean; these self-torture techniques must feel good to him.
- Passive-Aggressive Pam: is friendly when you meet in the hall but watch out if you need something done. She is the type that never answers your calls, memos or e-mails, no matter how many candy bars you leave on her desk.
- Political Animal Peter: rarely answers questions directly for fear of having to make decisions that could alienate anyone else at company---including the janitor.

- Drama King Dave: feels so inferior that ranting and raving in the middle of the hall is the only way he can feel powerful—take cover Rambo!

Oh, of course there is the boss (typically of the opposite sex but not always) who happens to call you up one day asking you to defend him in a sexual harassment case. Yep. I'll never forget the day I was sitting at my new desk, at my new office, in my very new job of two weeks. I had just been transferred to an office in one of the most beautiful cities in the world—San Francisco.

The phone rang and it was my old boss. The one that had helped me get the new job I was so happy about. The one I was so GRATEFUL to that I'd do anything for him. Well, *almost* anything. When I heard his voice, my heart jumped into my belly and I started to perspire. Then I became curious. *Was he going to take back the promotion? Would I have to go back home and give up this great new job?* Then I became angry. *Hadn't I served enough time under his tutelage?!* Then I regretted answering the call.

I clutched my pen fearfully —nearly squirting ink all over my *new* desk and computer, as I listened to the ex-boss's dilemma. As it turned out, some 20-yearold new female employee had taken his casual flirting a bit too seriously and had filed charges against the guy. He was asking that I take his side if any legal-types called.

Any semblance of womens' lib teachings quickly flew out the window as I feared for my paycheck. I was pissed at the Baby Prima Donna who was ruining my new life in paradise. After moving my earthly goods 400 miles to a new city, I wasn't feeling too socially conscious! (Mind you, I *have* been on the receiving end of slime-in-the-workplace and I know how difficult that is, so please bear with me here.)

Should I hang up now? Should I begin to talk in Croatian and pretend to be a different person than the one who picked up the line a minute before? Should I get down on my knees and pray for a quick trip that would take me out of the country for at least six months?

Former Girl Scout that I am, I decided to try none of these tactics and simply face the music. I remembered: *This was the second sexual harassment case I was asked to defend an executive in— I should be used to them by now.* You really have to keep an eye on these boss people. You never know what they'll get into next.

And you think your superiors are bad, what about your subordinates? I've been in middle management for a while now and

I've also had my own business. I have endured the experience of having others work for me. It's ever so interesting.

Way back in the early eighties I worked out of my Venice Beach charming-but-cramped two bedroom home. Now those were the days...Getting up at 6:30 a.m., putting on my business suit and walking down the hall to begin my work day... *Ugh! What was I thinking?! I must have been insane!*

Hmm...well...back to subordinates. I hired a student from the local university to help me out a few hours per week. Nothing heavy. Filing, typing, making sales phone calls to vicious homeowners during the dinner hour...(Just kidding!)

Anyway, one day Becky and I were working in the home office, doing whatever we did on Wednesday afternoons and she started to put away her pen and papers. It was only 4:00 PM and she usually stayed until 5:30 PM. "Uh, Amy, I need to leave early today." Yes, I allow my helper bees to address me by my first name even if MADAM YOUR HIGHNESS AMY sounds a lot better. I'm so liberated!

"Oh, Becky. I would have appreciated a little bit of warning ahead of time, but if it's very important, an emergency or something, I guess it's okay." I responded, rather miffed.

"Well, it's not exactly an emergency, Amy."

"Really, Becky? Go on." I started counting to ten.

"Well, it was such a nice day today, and..."

"And, WHAT, Becky?" Steam was starting to emerge from the top of my curly head as I tried to control my rising temper.

"And since you live right here at the beach, we thought that..."

"GO ON BECKY"*...is this because I only pay her $2.73 per hour?* I wondered as I fumed.

"It's just that my boyfriend, Ed, and I want to go to the beach today. So he's downstairs waiting for me right now."

THAT did it. *No five cent raise for this chick! And after all I had done for her!* (Well...give me a minute, I'll come up with something....) *She was betraying my good will! Playing on the beach instead of helping me file. How disrespectful! How ungrateful!! The youth of today!* At twenty-eight years old I was starting to sound like my dad.

Then there was Dictatorial Donna. This middle-aged gal was very bright, detested her menial job as the department secretary and had a bit of a chip on her shoulder. Perhaps you've worked with personnel like this. They tell YOU what to do. Especially when they're feeling the most insecure about being a lackey to twenty other corporate slaves. One day Donna summoned me into her office to explain how disappointed she was with my behavior.

Why couldn't *I* do this and that project? Didn't I understand how busy she was with....*With WHAT?* I mused. *More important versions of scut work? WHAT'S WRONG WITH THIS PICTURE?* Why did she think she could push me around like that?!

Could it be that I gave her gifts every little time she helped me with a significant office task? Was it the 20 stuffed teddy bears I have sitting in my cubicle? Or was it the fact that I was the one who passed out hats and noisemakers, threw on an apron and volunteered to serve the cake every time someone in the department had a birthday? Now that I think of it, perhaps my image around the place had become a bit too much like a cross between Donna Reed and a character on Sesame Street.

<u>How to Handle Humans-From-Hell That You See Everyday At the Office:</u>

- Develop laryngitis often so you will have to be selective about who you wish to speak with.

- Listen to comedy tapes before, during and after work to help laugh off the absurdities you encounter with others during the course of the day.

- Buy two large nerf-bats. One for pummeling your colleagues or bosses (in the safety of your own home and mind of course), the other for pummeling yourself for taking the job in the first place.

- Take a class in How to Handle Difficult People at least five times a year.

- Consider changing your career to the kind that involves working only with machines.

- Wear ear plugs to work; only remove them when absolutely necessary.

Chapter 5:
Project by Project They'll Keep Holding On: Office Tasks as We Know and Love Them

The beach was a misty gray that morning in Oxnard, California. Frothy waves were pushing against the deserted shore. I gazed from the second-story window of our honeymoon getaway onto the peaceful scene below, nursing my cup of coffee. My new husband lay gently sleeping in the king sized bed adjacent to my chair. After a few minutes I got back into bed and snuggled close to my handsome groom. Placing my supple lips next to his soft, fleshy ear lobe I whispered, "Honey, I've got to go back to work." Then I picked up my calculator and pencil and headed for the desk at the other side of the room, grumbling all the way.

"What?!" you ask. "She's on her *honeymoon* and doing work?" Well, it wasn't that bad—but almost.

Hubby Number One and I were given use of a friend's parents' oceanside home for a wedding present a few weeks after we were married. As it turned out, the weekend we were gifted with this Shangri-La I had to work. Some MAJOR report had to be finished, a million copies made and bound (or so it seemed) by Monday. What really kills me is that I can't remember the nature of the project; only the headache I endured getting it done.

That's Corporate America.

Corporate work projects are like bad bubble gum. Just when you think you're free for an hour or even a day to 'regroup' and do all those things you *never* have time for— like returning calls, cleaning up your desk, breathing, thinking and smiling at the people you verbally abused the week before because you were so stressed out over the darn project —then BAM! *It* reappears. That project you hoped you'd never see again; stuck to the bottom of your shoe. No matter how hard you struggle to free yourself it just gets stickier and stickier and attaches itself to other parts of your anatomy.

Back in the late Eighties I worked for a large computer products reseller. I was charged with implementing a sales incentive program for franchise store owners that sold a certain amount of widgets. When things didn't go right and the check did not arrive in the mail for these hard-working entrepreneurs, I was supposed to fix it. Each irate store owner became a separate item on my *To Do* list.

One case took a series of telephone calls to smooth things out. After several days of conversations with the store owner and several tête-à-têtes with my buddies in accounting, I thought we'd gotten things right. The file was put away in my personal drawer marked "Completed Projects that I Hope to Hell I Never See Again." *Ahhhhh.* That felt good.

Sure enough six weeks later the phone rings and it's Mr. Ripped Off Store Owner. He's back with a related problem to the problem I thought we fixed! Despairingly, I pulled out the previously buried file, wiped away the two inches of dust, along with my tears, and opened it. Some projects just refuse to die. Regardless of prayer.

Then there are the projects that mysteriously lose their *raison d'être* somewhere between the time you start them and the time you— in a state of frustration, burn-out and relief— hand over the completed work to your boss.

JUST A MINUTE,
DEAR...ONE LAST
REPORT TO E-MAIL!
Elena '98

I was asked to "handle" —which also means, "Complete-Or-You're-Back-On-The-Streets", babe— one work project that required the cooperation of two product managers. These two managers did not work directly for me so, of course, did not have to listen to what I said. After much hand-holding, bribery, sweet talk, planning, schedule juggling (one of the managers was out of town) and rewrites, the project was DONE—my favorite four letter word. Or so I thought.

I ran excitedly into my boss's office one sunny afternoon, project paperwork in hand. I was so glad to be rid of this assignment that had been hanging over my head for months like the huge alien spaceship in the movie *Independence Day.* As I gleefully handed the file to my boss he sheepishly thanked me and said "Uh... we actually discussed this project with the Regional Director of Sales and he's not sure he wants it to go to his staff after all."

What? I'm thinking as I feel my blood pressure rise. *Perhaps I heard you wrong. You're telling me that after two and a half months of agonizing over this project and coercing people that don't even work for me (since no one works for me, remember?) to do an extensive amount of work so that a department that none of us belong to can enjoy the benefits, the project is NO LONGER NEEDED? Please pass me my Uzi— I'm feeling the need to kill somebody!*

My boss was saying something about "Well, I'll check again to see what we want to do with this information," but I could barely hear him over my Internal War Machine. I just remember smiling innocently and backing slowly out of the office, arms straight at my sides to avoid punching the door on my way out.

In the Ideal World, your boss assigns you to do a project. You do it, your boss approves it and it goes out to some appropriate audience group—i.e., customers, finance department, cafeteria staff, whatever. Easy. In the Corporate World there is this thing called the "approval process." In one of my corporate functions I was asked to write a timely document for use mostly by sales and marketing people. Fine. Doing the research and writing the thing was simple. Getting the thing out the door was unbelievably complicated. But believe it!

I can take it when my boss offers a "few editing comments." Those same few editing comments from eleven other people is another story. Have you ever tried to incorporate ideas and grammatical "corrections" from several people in multiple departments that by nature do not agree on anything? It's like juggling five different plates made of Jello™. After getting signatures from marketing, product management and engineering reps for that project I seriously considered: *next shall I ask the janitor for his approval?* To top it off, after doing this whole Forty-Day Journey Through the Desert of Approvals, the "timely" information was practically obsolete!

That's Corporate America.

The next time you're going to start a work project there here are some helpful hints to help you get through the process:

<u>Five Project- Handling Tips for the Moderately Sane Corporate Employee</u>

- Bring one of your favorite pillows into your office. Keep it there for those times you'll be banging your head against the desk in utter frustration, while trying to finish a project.

- Carry three legal pads of paper with you every time you go to see your boss for work assignments. One is for the project description he/she gives you in the five minutes you meet; the other two are for the REAL project description that includes a listing of people whose help you'll need— or you're dead meat— and a time line of specific tasks. I warn you—it will be longer than the timeline between Columbus' journey to America and landing men on the moon!

- Stock up on aspirin. The "value- sized" bottle, next to the container marked "Ketchup for Millions" at your local supermarket, is just about right.

- Cancel your favorite social plans for the next six weeks. You'll need three of those to simply figure out what your boss actually wants you to do on the project. The next three can be used for doing it.

- Buy a container of table salt and place it in the middle of your desk—assuming you can find the middle with all the papers you may have stacked there. This is to remind you to take everything with a grain of salt as you trudge down the muddy road toward Project Completion. It can also be helpful when you buy a Breakfast Burrito from the Roach Coach and it needs a little extra spice.

Chapter 6:
The Office Party: How I Learned All I Need to Know about Radicchio Without Bothering to Ask

Someone was murdered on the 101 freeway. Did you hear? They shut down the whole darn freeway! Traffic was backed up for hours!

You can use all kinds of lettuce in salads these days. I like raddichio, arugula and endive. Sometimes I like to throw in peanut butter chips!

Oh yeah. We used to steal bottles of wine at my last job. I worked for a five star restaurant in Denver. After those big corporate holiday parties we used to get blitzed on leftover booze!

The office party. How delightful. You meet such interesting and high quality people. I have been attending such painful events for nearly two decades now and luckily, they're getting better. The reason? I only talk to people I like, drink mineral water and leave before 9:00 PM.

I've determined that there are three distinct types of office social events: Parties Held During the Day (a.k.a. Parties Without Alcohol); Parties *With* Alcohol; Parties that are Not Allowed to Exist.

Parties Held During the Day

This first type of event is often held during the day. Reasons can include birthdays, fund raiser kick offs, quarterly luncheons for no apparent reason other than to Reward the Slaves, someone's retirement, someone's departure by choice (notice that companies don't usually sponsor luncheons when someone gets canned), or to celebrate some Hallmark-deemed holiday like Bosses' Day. There is typically food at these seemingly innocuous get-togethers. And that, believe me, is the highlight of the event.

If a large group of people— say, the whole company is invited— then as people filter in, several small groups begin to form along the outer edges of the room. Like clumps of roses on a large white sheet cake. If you do not find someone you know at these events, you end up wandering aimlessly around the room, lukewarm soda in hand. Or, you spend the whole time befriending a large bowl of popcorn on the main food table.

Yeah, corporate parties can be so much fun.

The other kind of corporate gig is the smaller, department variety in which twenty or so people gather around foodstuffs and try to make small talk. And embarrassingly small it is. Intelligent adults that make important business decisions all day suddenly become nasty kindergartners.

I remember one such birthday gathering in which several long skinny candles were provided for the cake. A nice colleague of mine struggled to light these yuppie tapers with a Bic cigarette lighter—which believe me—it is not easy. As he persisted in this near impossible task, the not-so-grateful birthday boy exclaimed in the rudest voice imaginable "What are you DOING Steve?!"

He's trying to light the candles for YOUR birthday cake, you knucklehead! Can we please show a little gratitude here?!

I'm learning to love those uncomfortable silences between people while they munch on some overpriced birthday sweet while trying think of something clever to say. Well, *I* could think of something to say! It would sound like this: *Why did our department spend a lot of money on a* tres chic *birthday torte when I just got a measly five percent raise?*

And if office events aren't uncomfortable enough, slap the holiday theme on them and I'm really ready to run for cover.

I once attended a corporate Halloween Party at which I was pleasantly surprised. At this particular business-sponsored bash, only a few people were wearing costumes and the whole thing was pretty low-key. As I floated between company cliques, sipping fruit punch I had scooped from a smoking bowl (dry ice gives this effect when placed in cool liquid) and trying to find a safe place on which to perch for a few minutes, in walks the Devil himself. Yes— it was Shy Stan the Engineer Man, dressed in bright red tights and a bright red leotard. The whole group fell silent as we gazed at this tall, thin bespectacled man in a somewhat revealing getup. Then, tenuously a few of us went over to Stan to compliment him. Mostly women. The guys were still in a state of shock as their nerdy colleague got all the attention. (One male colleague later confessed that Stan had asked him for help 'zipping up' the leotard in the Men's Room minutes before which was a rather new experience for Colleague Chris.) I thought the event was wonderfully refreshing! A brave soul had finally appeared at a Corporate affair that *I* was attending. Usually I would just hear about these types of costumes after the fact.

I felt special. I felt like there was a corporate comrade out there, with guts, and I had finally met him. My years of feeling weirder than everyone else had finally ended. Then, within minutes, I felt so envious of this guy that I didn't need any green fright mask— I had my very own! Why hadn't *I* been the one brave enough to wear a SuperWoman costume among the masses? Huh? Why was I just another corporate weasel trying to look like everyone else. Ten years of expensive psychotherapy and I was *still* trying to fit in. I wanted to twist this Satan in Satin's tights around his neck and obliterate our anti-superhero right then and there! It was a scarier Halloween party than I originally thought.

Parties With Alcohol

There there are the parties with booze. Otherwise known as breeding grounds for sexual harassment charges.

I'll never forget one such event when the Vice President of Sales, a regularly gregarious guy, got a little too friendly. First he stepped—or is that sloshed?—over to say hello and practically fell on top of me as I was politely introducing him to my husband. Then after righting himself he extended his right hand to shake John's hand and placed his left one on the top of my back. As he continued to make unpleasant small talk with my husband he creepily slid his hand down my back to the top of my butt.

UGH!! Gross! ! I thought. This makes Boss Number Three with inappropriate behavior toward women. Can I pick 'em or what? I could see the lights of my attorney's eyes flashing in front of me. Luckily, a short time after that party a female colleague did press sexual harassment charges against the guy and saved me a mess of paperwork!

At another such party a typically shy engineering type guy—and a member of my department—insisted on giving me a hug at our company Christmas party. I guessed the personality change was not due to a Gestalt group the night before. It was an innocent embrace—not too different from the one I'd received from a female coworker moments before— but it was a quick reminder that people CHANGE when they've had something other than Seven Up™. What I want to know is why can't these over-friendly folks just quietly pass out like I used to in my drinking days? It's so much more polite!

And then there was the Chuck and Charlotte Incident. Charlotte was a lovely thirty-something woman with whom I worked at one company. She and her husband Chuck were at the company holiday party one year. John and I had enjoyed their company during the early part of the evening. Well, something happened between the "early part" and about 11:00 PM when we headed out.

As we approached the downtown parking garage where we left our Honda Accord several hours before, I noticed Charlotte and her husband embracing near the kiosk. "Can you look at that, Honey? How sweet! They must really be in love!" I said to my unimpressed spouse. Then as we approached the happy honeymooners, I noticed something was a bit off. Charlotte and Chuck were in the love-struck pose I thought I saw from a distance but there as one thing missing: Charlotte's feet were barely touching the ground. In addition, she was laughing—or was that crying?—hysterically into his new silk Armani tie. Apparently *she'd* tied on one too many on that night. (Eleven tequilas I heard later from the party animal herself. That'll do it!)

The You-Can't-Have-a-Party Party

What with all the rightsizing, downsizing and generally creating hordes of depressed unemployed professionals these days, many corporate entities are not having Christmas or Holiday or Whatever-Politically-Correct-Term-You-Want-to-Use parties anymore. There is a company Party Patrol that stalks around the building seeking out any form of holiday festivity to snuff out. Employees must hide any cards or gifts they receive from colleagues, refrain from wearing red and green and keep all holiday joy to a minimum. No unnecessary laughing or giggling and definitely not around the topic of *...shhhh...Christmas.*

I'm sure you've also heard about those pathetic replacements to traditional Yuletide festivities:

- Pot-luck lunches for employees only: How much Jello™ salad can one eat?

- Department lunches at fast-food restaurants: Extra chicken nuggets for everyone!

- Kids-only events with Santa Claus: Bribing the little ones so the employees won't complain. The oldest trick in the book!

And we mustn't forget about the schizophrenic company. Last year we attended a large extravaganza in one of these large public facilities which is normally used for elephant fashion shows or something. It's that BIG. There were 3000 people there, two floors of hot hors'doevres, photographers, live bands with dance floors and a sumptuous buffet. It was wonderful!

This year, however, my husband's firm will throw the Christmas Party That You Can't Have party. I guess the elephants needed the facility.

How to Avoid Holiday Parties And Still Get Credit for Going

- Find out where your neighbor or best friend works and where their office holiday party will be held. Crash that party and pretend that you're a new employee. Being around other peoples' colleagues can't be all that bad!

- Make an appearance at the party long enough to win any prize or eat any food they may give out: not both. Keep your stint under 20 minutes. That way you'll be able to talk about something notable at the party come Monday, without the trauma of staying the entire evening.

- Volunteer to help decorate and set up. People will be so tired of seeing you they will hardly miss you when you slip out 10 minutes before "showtime."

- Develop a fake sprained—not broken—ankle. Come to the party on crutches. That will give you an excuse not to wear an expensive, sexy gown and keep you well-protected from groping hands or pleas for dancing. The next Monday you will be miraculously healed and dance all the way to the office, happy that you made it through yet *another* office Christmas party.

- Change your religion to the kind that doesn't let you celebrate *anything.*

Chapter 7:
Temporary Parole: Seminars, Conferences, Trade Shows and the Like

I was freezing. Draped in my thick black coat, hand cupped around a worn Styrofoam cup of hot tea, I sat with teeth chattering. As the clock ticked on I strained to see the materials that were shoved in front of me moments before--- the room was very poorly lit. As I glanced around all I saw were hundreds of other zombies just like me. Dressed in black or gray, unable to see and barely able to hear since the acoustics in the facility were so poor. Perhaps the cold had already killed most of my comrades and they were simply frozen upright, dead in their chairs.

A recent nightmare? A prisoner-of-war camp in Antarctica? Heck no! It was a half-day conference I attended last Friday!

In my early days as a member of the corporate slave set I used to perceive attending a seminar, trade show or conference like a paid day off. I got to learn something different, meet new and interesting people and eat free food. It was fun and something I looked forward to. Note the past tense.

Nowadays when my boss asks me to attend an outside event, I break out in a rash. *Will I have the right clothing to sustain the weather conditions? Should I bring my own food to avoid salmonella, or worse, an attack of hypoglycemia because the food they have is inedible? Do I have travel out of town or can I sleep in my own bed?* We're talking about basic *survival* here folks.

I remember a one-day conference that was held in a dark room— all day. The place was so dimly lit you could barely see the EXIT signs. It was also so large you could only see the person on the stage if you squinted. It was like seeing Vincent Price in *The Fly* with a big booming voice broadcast over a microphone. All audio and very little visual. After scoping out this venue I decided my quest for the day would be to find daylight. I knew I had seen it on the way in that morning on the train. I was sure it could be found again.

7:00AM - INTRODUCTION
10:00AM - CONTENT
LUNCH - SOMETIME BEFORE Y2K
CONCLUSION: ??
Z-Z-Z-Z
ZZZ

At the first break, around 10:30 AM, I needed to use the bathroom. Since my eight and a half minutes were quickly used up I knew the lunch break would be my big opportunity. To be sure, two hours later I was raring to go. *Sun! Wind! Fresh Air! Wait for me, I'm a-comin! Just a quick minute before the lunch break is all I need.* But then I heard it over the loud speaker: "Lunch will begin in exactly three and a half minutes in the Petal Room on the Mezzanine. Just exit the northwest doors, cross the sixteenth floor to the elevators on the right. Go down six floors and go out into the hall. Make a left and step on first bank of escalators you come to. Take them to the fourth floor and look for the room marked Banquet Room 322. Enter that room but don't stay there. Just keep walking. Lunch will be served at the back of Banquet Room 222 which is down the steps, out the side doors and to the left. This message will not be repeated. Bon Appetit!"

WAIT! WAIT! You're going too fast! I have to write this down! Now, how am I going to get my Real Air?!

My skin was turning the color of the uncomfortable gray chairs we sat on. My breathing had become shallower and shallower and I could barely remember my name. After sustaining myself on ice water and peppermints for the previous two hours I was clinging to a thin lifeline. *Food or air? Air or food?* I had to think quickly. Since I'm prone to hypoglycemia I decided I better head for lunch and postpone my date with Mother Nature until the 4:00 PM break.

Mother Nature, bless her heart, never forgave me for that. By the time I made it outside the building it was raining cats and dogs.

I'll never forget one trade show I attended that was more like Disneyland—or was it the House of Horrors?—than a business forum. It was one of those exhibits held in a huge convention center. Concrete walls and floors. Escalators long enough to accommodate the crowds at Hoover Dam. Enough human beings to make the cast of *The Ten Commandments* look tiny. Not particularly cozy.

At one such venue I attended I decided that I needed an apple juice. Finding refreshment at a large trade show can be agonizing— like searching for an oasis in a desert, hiking up a steep mountain, or walking through a mine field—and this day wasn't any different. I had hoofed it around the floor along with the masses and, after three hours of such torture, that's what I wanted. I quickly remembered that concession stands are often tucked away at these events so I decided to get crafty. I did a quick scan of the very congested exhibition floor, and saw nothing but signage and carnage, so I asked a nearby human being where food could be purchased. After being pointed in what I hoped was the correct direction I made a beeline toward the place.

I was undaunted in my mission. I stopped at nothing. I looked at no one. I had made it this far and I didn't want to break my good record. The angels were with me, luckily, and after a few challenging minutes I had arrived. I had made it to the All Hailed Concession Area in one piece. In the middle of congratulating myself for my fine navigation work, I easily spotted my sparkling juice behind a tall glass refrigerator door and grabbed a six ounce bottle in the shape of a chubby apple. Cool and refreshing-looking, my juice smiled back at me, ready to be gulped. What a treat! As visions of tantalizing soft drink commercials returned to me, I turned around, looking for a place to pay. That's when I saw it. It was horrible.

More frightening than the Bogey Man. More loathsome than Jack the Ripper. More disgusting than the figure in *The Blob*. It was the *line*. In my haste to reach my goal, I had forgotten that other people also get thirsty and hungry at trade shows. Lots of them.

In addition to being a struggle for physical survival, trade shows can also be lonely. At one show I visited years ago I felt an invisible fortress take shape around my body as I began my slow walk around the booths. Remember Abe Lincoln at Disneyland?

That's how I felt as I nodded my head up and down, smiling at the many faces that passed before me.

The lights surrounding the booths were piercingly bright and the variety of sounds at the show bounced around the concrete walls like pinballs gone haywire. Before long I realized one important thing: I was in pain. To top it off I felt a little bit claustrophobic. My heartbeat began to quicken and I forced myself to take a few long, deep breaths. *Stop it Amy! You can't feel breathless in a 300,000 square foot facility with 400 windows! Proceed, Soldier!*

I decided to seek temporary refuge at a booth where the natives seemed friendly. Within minutes I spotted a brown-haired woman sitting at a table with particularly long legs. (The table, not the woman.) She wasn't one of those intimidatingly beautiful women in short, tight Chanel business suits and three inch heels—one of those ladies you suspect may have been hired as a customer attraction piece, otherwise known as a Booth Babe.

She wore little makeup and her hair was slightly disheveled. Kind of like me by this time. She wore a nice green crystal around her neck. I had an interest in metaphysical stuff. This relationship could actually work. *Hooray!* I thought as I pranced over to see her. A possible friend in the electronic jungle. A buddy with whom to connect and regroup. An excuse to rest my already tired feet.

I walked over to New Age Gal and introduced myself, asking what product her company offered. She smiled and handed me brochures on the software her firm published. She even told me about a sweepstakes the company was sponsoring and asked if I wanted to enter my name. I was in a precious moment of Trade Show Heaven. I had found a *real* person to talk to.
I could win a trip to Hawaii. My feet felt great.

I filled out the contest registration form and continued to ask more questions about her company's product. I thought the graphic artists in my department might be interested. I even asked my new friend if I might contact her for more information and asked for her first name.

Then it happened. The worst of the worst. The unspeakable. The crystal necked lady simply pointed to a phone number on a brochure and claimed "Just call this number; anyone there can help you." *Anyone there can help you* —I couldn't believe my ears! We had just spent a lifetime together, shared intimate moments, smiled and laughed together. And this was the best she could do? *What was I? Chopped liver?*

After our connection—OK, it *was* only five minutes—she was leaving me to fend for myself. An innocent lamb in the midst of all those hungry wolves! The hand that I thought had been extended was callously jerked away. There I was, feeling lost and alone again. In the Fun House at the County Fair, with no one to guide me.

Without looking back, I fled the trade show, heart in hand and checkbook in pocket. I needed one of those Chanel suits. And fast.

<u>Conference and Seminar Survival Tips for the Nineties and Beyond</u>

- Beg, cajole and plead with your colleagues to go to the event in your place.
- Stock up on granola bars, M&Ms and/or fresh fruit—never depend on the quality, quantity or timing of the rations at public these events.
- Purchase two sets of hand warmers—the kind you can buy for skiing—and a battery-charged sock warmer. When your toes start to turn blue inside those flimsy panty hose, you'll thank me for this.
- Look for any and all sources of natural light; this will be a unique offering that you won't want to share with anyone else, when that cold, dark, hermetically sealed room starts to get to you.

- Escape to the hotel lobby for ten precious minutes after you've wolfed down the rubber chicken, 4000-calorie chocolate cake and mediocre coffee you're served at lunch. This is a *crucial* survival technique due to the following: when you first enter the building in which the event is held, an infrared personal locator device will be secretly implanted in your left shoulder. It will emit a loud siren-type noise if you attempt to open any doors to the *real* outside world.

Chapter 8:
Phantom of the Office: Politics Prevail Over All

One Friday afternoon, I was sitting at one of my 'temp' desks, minding my own business when the telephone rang. "Hi, Amy. This is Fred from TempPower." Sure, I knew Fred! He was the delightful man who had placed me in numerous temporary jobs over the prior several months. He was the man with whom I could laugh and shoot the breeze. The one I could fantasize about.

Yes, I often imagined getting up real close to Fred, raising my arms, and... pummeling him with my fists while yelling at the top of my lungs, "I don't want any more temp jobs! I'm an M.I.T. grad, for God's sake! Is this why I got into debt for $10,000 a year? Can't you see I need a real job?!"

During this time of my life I was on the brink of near-destitution (my boyfriend did feed me, bless his soul) and jobs from TempPower helped keep me in the style to which I was accustomed.

Alive.

"So, what's up Fred?" I responded, as my heart jumped into my stomach. It's not a good thing when you're fulfilling a temporary job that's supposed to last three months and you get a call from the agency at the end of week two.

"Well, it turns out today is your last day there at Company XYZ." "Last day! I thought this was a long term assignment. " I exclaimed, trying not to sound too hysterical—and failing. "What happened, Fred?!"

Office politics. That's what happened.

A few days before this ominous call I had what I considered to be an important conversation with a colleague of mine at Company XYZ. We were resolving a minor conflict and building a little more trust. In the middle of our meeting, in blasts a department Director announcing, "Amy, you have a phone call on line three. It's Bill Jensen."

Bill Jensen? Who's that? I wondered. My position at XYZ involved talking with a lot of different people and putting together bids for product sales. The name Bill Jensen rang no bells for me so I said to Ms. Director, "Well, Jan and I are just finishing up an important discussion. Could you please tell Bill I'll get back to him in ten minutes? Thanks."

That, my friends, was the death knell. Apparently, Bill Jensen was one of the company's Regional Sales Managers. Who knew? I *didn't* memorize the organization chart the first day I got there. Apparently, when I received the call, regardless of what I was doing, I was supposed to be rude to my colleague (of a lower rank than old Billy of course), jump out of my chair, tear over to my desk at the speed of an Indy 500™ racecar and bow and scrape my way to the phone. Just in time to receive some dumb question from MISTER Jensen who I would probably never meet in person during my entire life.

Why? Office politics of course.

Those insipid unwritten rules in an organization that dictate who sits down first and where, who gets birthday cake at an office party and who gets to open their mouth before everybody else when participating in a long-distance conference call. I suppose these rules also pertain to who gets to use the potty first when you're traveling with your boss on an airplane with only one bathroom that claims, "Vacancy."

The bad news is that office politics is everywhere. The good news is that the culprits are easy to spot. They are more ferocious than King Kong. More despicable than killer bees. More scary than boa constrictors in heat.

These beastly beasts are PA's. Otherwise known as Political Animals. To ensure continual paychecks it is wise for corporate entities to remember the following characteristics about PAs:

- PAs are very loyal—to themselves.
- PAs talk incessantly and never answer a question directly. In fact, PAs are very creative: they try to place blame on the person asking the question rather than answer it. In fact, they'd rather *die* than answer a question for fear of making a mistake.
- PAs have PhD's in Paranoia.
- PAs have the same middle name the world over: Ego.
- PAs have the same mantra: "FUD"— which stands for Fear, Uncertainty and Doubt.

I remember one job where I was politely expelled because the guy I worked for was chums with the department head. (I never liked that expression. It always brings to mind a giant HEAD walking around spouting out orders: "This is your department

...JUST PUT THE REPORT OVER THERE IN THE CART, HON.

HEAD! I have no arms or legs and no way to propel myself around but you must listen to me because I'm the HEAD of our department!") Expelled, even though I worked my rear end off and produced much better work than my superior—but, hey, any healthy corporate slave knows that stellar work ranks much *lower* than office politics.

In fact, Mr. Boss and Mr. Head often lunched together. Yep. They were good buddies. They probably golfed and fished together as well. To put it plainly: I DIDN'T HAVE A CHANCE. When push came to shove (which is what I wanted to do to these Bobsey Bosses), I was dead meat.

"Are you sure you really fit in here, Amy?" the HEAD asked me one day. *Why can't they just be totally honest?* I silently beckoned to the universe. I would have appreciated a simple, "Your work is great, your boss is threatened and you're out of here, babe."

"Well, Bob, if you think people with ethics and very high work standards fit in here, then yes I do." I innocently replied. Even as I tried my very best Little Bo-Peep impersonation pictures of severance checks danced around in my head. I felt a slight case of nausea coming on as I envisioned the long line at the unemployment office. I was no match for the good old boys' club of white collar execs, but I'd be damned if I wasn't going to go out trying.

That's the "P" word. Life in Corporate America would be much nicer if, when you're issued your employee benefit package, you were also given an Office Politics Detector Patch. Like the kind they give you to prevent seasickness or suppress the urge to smoke. After signing up for your favorite HMO, some friendly Human Resources person would gently implant a small square patch under one of your armpits. Each time you come within 36 inches of a political encounter at the office, you'd start to feel a little itchy under there. You would then have the opportunity to politely excuse yourself and run off to the bathroom where you could scratch to your heart's desire and plot your next course of action.

Why under the armpit? Office politics are so smelly, you know.

Seven Rules for Playing the Political Game at Work

- Whip out your old college book from Psychology 101. Look up the word 'ego.' Memorize the definition.

- Scope out your immediate supervisorial structure: who reports to whom; who *really* reports to whom. Remember: titles mean nothing.

- Watch a minimum of three daytime soap operas (you can tape them when you're away at work). The plot themes are uncannily like the interactions that go on at the office.

- Go slow for the first six months of employment. Spend half your time talking with colleagues and bosses and the other half doing your work. You *will* have to give up your social life for these six months, because you'll be at the office so darned much, but it could save you in the long run.

- Listen to an audio tape set about Image and Business Etiquette. (I'm serious.)

- Take a comedy writing class at your local community college. You'll be getting some wonderful material just from your daily interactions at work.

- Remember, it's just that: a prized performance, or better yet, a game.

Chapter 9: Business Travel: Leavin' On An Airplane Don't Know If I'll Be Back Again 'Cause I Could Get a Job Offer From the Guy Sitting Next to Me

"Oh no! I forgot my drivers' license!" I exclaimed to the man standing behind the counter. The tears welled up in my eyes and I saw my life flash before me: Loss of job. Life as an L.A. Bag Lady. Death from lack of food. "You see, Sir, I'm supposed to be doing one-on-one interviews with residential sales agents all over Tucson for this market research project I'm working on and I left my license in my other jacket because my husband and I went dancing last night and I needed it for I.D. I forgot to take it out and put it in my purse and I REALLY need a car and, and..." *Please God. Please God. I love my job. I can't afford to lose it. I'll do anything. Wash other people's cars. Listen to the evening news for a week. And, yes, I'll even cook dinner every once in a while. ANYTHING if you just get me a car!*

"I'm sorry, Ma'am, but I can't give you a rental car unless I see a copy of your drivers' license."

So much for the power of prayer when traveling for Corporate America.

I'll never forget those early days of traveling for work when I'd get all gussied up: business suit, stockings and heels, briefcase at my side, only to emerge from my flight, looking and feeling like an ice sculpture at last year's office Christmas party. Frozen solid. It took me 18 years of living in the Corporate Fast Lane to figure out that I needed to bring a pair of thick wool socks, a knitted hat and some mittens with me—and that was just to make it through the flight.

After one business trip to New York from San Francisco I went from cold plane to muggy cab to cold hotel room—in less than an hour. I had to lie in a warm tub for 20 minutes to simply balance out my biorhythms. I was probably the only person in New York City taking a hot bubble bath in the middle of June.

After surviving the plane, today's business traveler must then endure an equally hellish experience: finding one's luggage. By the time you drag yourself through the airport to the Baggage Claim section you've entirely forgotten which of the six large, oval metal conveyor belts your suitcase is supposed to emerge from. Was it Number 2? Or was it Number 5? And when you *have* seen the light—in the form of the name of your city flashing across the monitor— you realize that 98% of your fellow business flyers have the same cute little black Deals-On-Wheels suitcase.

Those on the outside think traveling for work must be fun. Little do *they* know. On my last business trip to San Diego, the following happened:

- I was told by the airport aide to look for a green and white shuttle bus to take me to my hotel. There were at least nine buses that fit that description, each going in different directions.

- When I checked into my hotel I discovered that my reservation wasn't good until the following night.

- Due to the kindness of many souls, I did get a room that night. When I finally made it up there, my stomach was growling loud enough to qualify me for a place at the zoo, in the Lions Section. I also discovered that the in-room dining department had just closed its dinner service. Potato chips and cocoa never tasted so good!

- The room I was granted was 5' by 10' with a bed that dropped down from the wall. I barely had enough room to get to the bathroom when I needed to pee in the middle of the night.

Then there are the traveling schedules we Corporate Comrades are expected to keep. Fly out Wednesday morning for a Wednesday afternoon meeting. Take the Red Eye flight back that night. Or was it the next morning? No wonder Corporate America is so messed up. How can anyone think after a round-trip flight like that?

I remember wobbling into the office after a 72 hour business trip back East. I don't know how I drove myself to the office that day, I was so tired. My clothes were disheveled, my coiffure qualified me for the Worst Bad Hair Day Ever contest and I needed to lean against a piece of office furniture in order to maintain my balance. The company probably lost more money that week due to my lack of productivity than what they saved in hotel fees.

I once had a colleague who flew out to London from San Francisco on a Tuesday and back home again on Saturday. In the same week. All that time in the air and he *still* had time for a trip to Harrods. At least he had his priorities right.

"SORRY I'M LATE, MY FLIGHT JUST ARRIVED."

Speaking of Saturdays, we can't forget—as much as I'd like to—the You-Really-Don't-Have-A-Life-So-Stay-Over-A-Saturday-Night-And-We'll- Knock-Some-Bucks-Off-Your-Fare fare. I don't see my husband enough as it is. You think I really want to fly out to some God-forsaken city—where I don't know a soul, and ruin my precious weekend just to save my company a few pennies? I think not. No wonder the divorce rate continues to soar in this country.

And what about the people we have to endure while traveling for The Man (or The Woman)? On one business trip from hell I had to endure loud conversations from drunken passengers, salami breath from the person sitting next to me, crying babies and snotty flight attendants. All this with only a ragged copy of the airline shoppers' catalog for company. I had left my precious paperback book in my garment bag which was being cryogenically preserved somewhere in the bowels of the plane.

A colleague of mine once spent his five hour return flight from a business trip writhing on the floor of the plane's mini-kitchen, as close to a bathroom as possible. Was it the nine days working at a trade show in a strange city that got him so sick? Or the plane flight itself?

Only one thing is known for sure. Business travel can really suck.

Speaking of trade shows, they are like portable cities these days. The last one I attended had 2000 attendees. The one before that had over 100,000. A former boss once attended a trade show where the town was so crowded with attendees that a taxi was nowhere to be found. After hiking three and half miles in his Florsheim loafers and Brooks Brothers suit, he and his buddy decided to take the transport of last resort: the city bus and here's what they heard: "Get the hell out of my way you jerk!" "Hey, I sat there first, you do-do brain!" "If you don't move that bag I'm gonna punch your lights out!" A relaxing experience for two weary business travelers, wouldn't you say?

Their transportation experience reminds me of the cab driver in New York City who aged me by at least two years. I had heard of this anthropological subgroup of humans but never experienced one. On the way to JFK airport from Manhattan, one sunny afternoon, I learned how to hit the floor of a taxicab in under than 20 seconds flat, say fifteen Hail Marys (which is not easy when you're Jewish) and refrain from vomiting up an expensive lunch. That ride made the rollercoaster at Six Flags amusement park look like a stroll down a country lane with Mary and her Little Lamb.

Crowded conference centers and tiny hotel rooms are joined by something else typical of business trips. Lack of food. I once attended a conference where continental breakfast was served between 7:15 and 8:00 AM. Not wanting to waste a minute of sleep, I arrived at the buffet table at 8:17 AM. Okay, I was late. But not overly so. I thought the conference producers would have pity on us latecomers and save a few morsels.

To my unpleasant surprise, the tables were being cleared away. Men and women in white coats were dusting off crumbs, stacking dirty coffee cups and putting away soiled dishes. I panicked and my empty stomach called out for mercy. *There's got to be something left— I'm only seventeen minutes late!* Then, by the grace of God, I saw it. Sitting on the edge of the long, nearly desecrated white-tableclothed buffet table—all by its lonesome: a lemon poppyseed muffin. As I reached over to grab that precious jewel away from the betraying hands of a hotel staffperson, I couldn't believe my bloodshot eyes. Horror-of-horrors, my muffin was already HALF-EATEN. Some heartless conference attendee had merely broken off one side of the pastry, leaving it on the table, unfinished, to torture me.

Like I said. Business travel is not all it's cracked up to be.

How to Survive Business Travel:

- Clone yourself and send your look-alike on the trip.

- Develop life-threatening allergies to the Top Ten plants that thrive in each major region of the U.S. and Europe.

- Get good drugs. That way you can sleep through the plane flight and half of the business meetings too.

- Bribe people you meet over the Internet to become your friends. That way you'll have folks to visit when you're in places like What-The-Heck, Washington and Thank-God-I'm-Only-Here-for-a-Day, Tennessee.

- Throw away your wristwatch. Everything will be later or earlier than you expect, so why get yourself in a tizzy?

Chapter 10: Getting a Job in Corporate America: Wouldn't Climbing Mount Everest be Easier?

I applied for a job as a customer service representative at a financial institution. It was my 114th job application in the past 3 months and I prayed for an easy time.

Do you own your own car?

So far, so good.

Do you have car insurance?

My God, I can smell my first paycheck.

Have you ever been convicted for a felony or misdemeanor?

Bye bye unemployment!

Have you ever been fired or asked to leave a position?

I experienced shortness of breath and felt a migraine coming on. *It can't be true, I thought. We were doing so well and then the Big Kahuna appears to ruin my day, my week, my life. Will I never be allowed to forget the time Frank the V.P. called me into his office to tell me,* " Uh, Amy, I think we have a chemistry problem here…" *Chemistry? Why are we talking beakers and flasks?! I thought we were in the real estate business!*

Looking back, I don't think I took that one real well. If you can actually make it to one, the interview is no piece of cake—for the candidate *or* the interviewer. A friend once relayed this to me: "So, I'm not five minutes into interviewing this guy and thinking, well, he's kind of quiet but not too bad and then KERTHUNK! His head drops on the desk like a 75— pound sack of potatoes and he starts to snore!" Job hunting can be tiring, you know.

There there was the interview story I heard about the candidate who pulled a tuna salad sandwich out of her briefcase and began chomping away when the clock struck twelve. You never know when you'll get your next meal when you're unemployed, so why take chances?

I also heard about the interviewee who didn't like the conference room he was brought to because it lacked windows. He demanded that he be moved before answering any questions. I didn't realize I had so many options. Over the past two decades I've been on countless job interviews and never once did I think of taking a nap, having a snack or dabbling in interior decorating.

Although, I did have a interview where I was asked to give a fifteen minute presentation on *anything.* Perhaps I should not have chosen the topic: "How to Turn Your Company Upside Down in Five Easy Steps."

The interview process is also tough because it's so unpredictable. The times you think to yourself, " This job's really not for me but I'll go for the interview practice," you end up staying for two days. Then there are the days you cancel all your plans because you assume, "I'm perfect for this gig! I better prepare myself to be at their office for awhile" and they practically throw you out with the morning trash after seventeen minutes.

Another fascinating element of interviewing, that might surprise you, is that you have to do it for temp jobs. One day for example, I got a call which went like this: "Hi Amy. This is Babs from Temp-All-Your-Life, Incorporated. You were in here yesterday."

My heart skipped a beat. *A possible JOB. Money. Clothes. Gas for my car. I could even get a haircut.* "Ah yes, Babs. I remember."

"...YES! YOUR RESUME IS EXCELLENT!"

"Well, Amy, we have a possible position for you. It's a long-term, temporary-but-could-be-permanent, but, in the meantime, short-term job."

"GREAT! I'll take it!" I was jazzed now. Visions of eating out in restaurants, again, danced around in my head. *McDonalds, here I come!*

"I'm sure I'd be perfect, Babs. Thanks ever so much. When do I start?"

"Amy, I appreciate your interest," replied Babs, "But, don't you want to know what you'd be doing? The salary? Location?"

"Uh—uh—sure, Babs. Of course those factors must be considered," I stammered sheepishly. *You've GOT to be kidding! I have been underemployed for six months. My resume is turning yellow along with my diplomas. I just gave up my car because I couldn't make the payments and I shop at Goodwill. You think I care where the money comes from?*

"And there's one more thing, Amy."

"Yes, Babs?"

"You have to interview for the position."

My bubble was burst. My dream was squashed. My parade was completely washed out. *For a mere six bucks an hour, I have to INTERVIEW? What has this world come to?* I thought as I took down the address.

There is another new phenomena in today's corporate world where people love to talk about interviewing. It's called the Outplacement Center. Trust me—these places are more like an *Outpatient* Centers for those that have been surgically removed from their previous place of employment. Slightly bloody, lots of depressed people and time on your hands.

Getting the word from your boss that your job (a.k.a. *you*) have been terminated is bad enough. When they send you to these human recycling centers for the Work-Weary-and-Really-Pissed-Off you know you've got it bad. On the outside, it seems that companies that ship their newly laid-off chicks to these institutions are good guys. They claim they want to help you endure the "life transition." You know. The one from Steady Paycheck to Sorry-Bob-But-You're-Headed-for-the-Poorhouse.

In reality, the folks at your soon-to-be former job are guilt-ridden as hell. As the middle manager of the Inhuman Resources Department hands you the letter which explains when and where the next Outplacement orientation takes place, he secretly prays, "*Please* don't sue me. I know you have three kids in college, two mortgages on your house and have just bought a new Mercedes which you will now have to give up...but PLEASE just take your nice little letter and go away quietly…No hard feelings I hope…."

Outplacement centers are to die for. Not literally, you hope. The curriculum at these centers is also not what you'd think. When I arrived at my first OC I thought, "Oh good. Some self-esteem building, hearing other peoples' war stories, New Age touchy-feely personal awareness exercises. What a great way to save money on therapy." Boy was I wrong! Being in that Outplacement Center was like enlisting in the Marines. You only get three minutes to tell your story and then the drill sergeant—I mean facilitator—gets right to the point.

"You are here for one thing and one thing only, people! GET THE INTERVIEW!"

"Stan, can we spend more time talking about our feelings of anger and…."

"GET THE INTERVIEW!"

"I was hoping to explore different career options…"

"GET THE INTERVIEW!"

"Do you think, Stan, we could do an occupational analysis test and…"

"I DON'T CARE IF YOU PEOPLE LIE, CHEAT OR DESTROY THE ENVIRONMENT, JUST—"

We know, we know…get the interview.

Getting the interview, however, is harder said than done. In fact, in some circles it's referred to as Mission Impossible. Once I was desperate for an interview at a well-known computer manufacturer. I just *knew* it was the place for me. So, when I saw the ad in the newspaper I sent in my obligatory cover letter and resume. I sat back to wait for the call from Human Resources asking me to come in for an interview. What I got, instead, was a rejection letter. You know, the kind that says "We appreciate your interest in our firm but do not have a position that meets your qualifications, yada, yada, yada."

No biggie. I've been through this before. It just means they have entered the data from my resume into their database along with 23,170 others. I'll just send them another one to refresh their memory of me. So, I sent in another cover letter and resume. *Piece of cake. That call should be coming any day now.*

Ten days later I was shocked to find yet *another* rejection letter in my mailbox from Big Banana Computer Company. *Hey! Don't these clowns know I went to M.I.T.? Okay, so I only have one year of experience for the job I'm interested in. Once they meet me, they'll see I'm the gal for them.*

The third cover letter and resume went out that day. It might not surprise you to know I've been called "stubborn" by friends and relatives. Personally, I prefer the words, "highly focused."

Six days later the bomb hit. You guessed it. Another letter just like the first two. *ALRIGHT—You're in for it now! When I get done with you, you'll be batter for muffins, breads and bagels.* Or I'll have a job. I spent a whole day formulating my three-pronged attack.

First: confirm the name on the three letters—Bob Smith, Vice President, Human Resources. Second: buy two blueberry muffins. Third: Get up at 4:30 AM so I can have enough time to meditate, get dressed, put on makeup and make it to Bob's doorstep by eight o'clock a.m., in spite of the southern California traffic. As dawn crested over the San Diego freeway the next day, muffins at my side, I planned my entry statement: "Hi! I'm Amy Weisman (maiden name) and I don't have an appointment but I know Mr. Smith will be delighted to see me." *Too Pollyanna.* "Hi! I'm Amy Weisman and I'm here to tell you why you MUST to hire me!"

A bit too Sarah Bernhardt. "Hello. I'm A. Weisman. The one you SOBs sent three rejection letters to and I'm here to TELL YOU JERKS THAT ...." *Oh well, I'm sure I'll think of something.*

I didn't get thrown out of Bob's office that morning. He even agreed to chat with me for thirty minutes. But all I ever got from the Big Banana was an empty bag of crumbs. And a few passed-over blueberries.

Five Sure-Fire Tips for Preparing for a Job Interview:

- Cleanse thyself. Taking a shower is a must to clean off all body parts. Beware, however, this innocent hygienic ritual can become part of a horror story when you're getting ready for an interview. You may find yourself praying: *Please, God, don't let me slip and break my neck! I've been out of work for over nine months and this is the SECOND interview I've been called for—please let me live. I still have to pay off my student loan from grad school!*

- Dress thyself appropriately. You may want to take the seminar entitled, "Interviewing Skills For the Downtrodden."

- Prepare thy portfolio. Job search experts say it's always a good idea to bring a backup copy of your resume and list of references to an interview. Print out your materials the night before to avoid the inevitable printer problems you would encounter on the big day. Believe me, these machines can sense when you're desperate and like to torture you by running out of toner or paper minutes before you must get in the car. Assume there will be at least one typo somewhere in your package.

That way you won't be crushed when your interviewer asks you about it.

- Arrive early. Bring a pair of tennis shoes to wear when you spend 35 long minutes strolling the parking lot timing your entrance. (When I was interviewing I walked around so many Bay Area parking lots the State Department of Transportation could have hired me as a part-time surveyor!)

- Be honest when filling out the job application form. But not TOO honest. Remember, you need to eat.

Chapter 11: Office Systems: Make Like a Cheese and Get Processed

New Hire. Rhymes with New Tire. It's what the Human Resources department labels new recruits. Like they have leprosy or something, HR gives new employees a label—New Hire—to keep them apart until they can be considered one of the clan.

I recall one New Hire orientation several years back. When I was told about the event by my new boss, I expected a large group of people, coffee and doughnuts, balloons and perky music playing in the background. Almost like a welcome party for new recruits. Instead, I got a quiet, dark room in an obscure corner of the building, one other human being, sipping on his morning coffee, and a stack of paperwork to fill a small warehouse. Were they going to interrogate me under a bright lamp or hook me up to wires for a lie detector test? Where were the balloons and cookies?

After slugging through a meager portion of the papers sitting on the table, a Human Resources rep appeared before my fellow inmate and me. She began a lengthy and boring diatribe about the Dos and Don'ts of working at the company: "You are entitled to 15 'paid time off' days. Otherwise known as PTO. You can take those for vacation, doctors' appointments, sick days and what not. You cannot roll them over to an upcoming year. You must take them all this year."

So, if I am very healthy and can't possibly afford to take a two week fancy vacation (on what you're paying me, fat chance), I have to feign illness to get the day off?! No wonder I read this headline just the other day: **Cheating At Work Blamed on Squeeze of Job Pressures: 48% Admit Ethics Lapses.**

"You will be evaluated in ninety days and put on probation until then." I felt like I had committed a crime but I didn't know for what. "Please fill out and sign Forms A-A6 and A7 on insurance, Forms 2-11-P and 3-11-P on our sexual harassment policy, Forms X-99-2 and X-88-2 on our travel and entertainment policy and Forms 00-GG-6, 00-XX-6 and 00-LL-3 for your 401K account. I'll be back in 5 minutes to collect them." *Is it too early to take a sick day?* I wondered.

Health insurance itself is a nightmare. Do I want Plan A with a $300 deduction, Plan B with a $200 deduction, Plan C with $75 deduction but no pharmaceuticals coverage or, lastly, Plan D with no deduction but also no doctor. Plan E is the U-PICK form of health care. See whatever quack you prefer, but pay full price.

When one company I worked with went public I had to hire a translator to help me interpret the stock options versus stock purchase plan documentation. And I have three college degrees!

In addition to the paperwork part of a New Hire Orientation, there are also training films to endure. You know, things like: *How to Survive Psychopathic Coworkers*; *How to Survive the Food at the Company Cafeteria*; *How to Do the Work of Five When You're Getting Paid Bupkis.* The content is usually boring and they don't even supply popcorn.

One time it took me over three weeks to place an order a new bookshelf my cube. First I had to find the Facilities Request Form on my computer. That took five days. Then I had to figure out how to fill it out. Another eight days. Then there was a holiday. Another four days. Then there was the waiting to hear from Facilities about my request. Another six days. Then there was correcting the mistake I made on the Facilities Request Form. Another four days. Then there was the backlog of the item at the bookshelf manufacturing plant. Another five days. By the time I got the darn thing we had moved to a new building and I didn't have room for it anyway!

In reality, office processes are not all that bad. Think of it this way. After you've made it through your New Hire orientation, you just have to complete your ***first*** full department birthday celebration, ***first*** communication-building workshop, your ***first*** one-on-one lunch with your boss after your 90 day probation period, your ***first*** one-on-one meeting with your boss after six months of work, your ***first*** one-on-one meeting with your boss after nine months on the job and your ***first*** annual performance review to before you get to pick your Year One anniversary gift from the K-mart catalog.

But fear not, only one of these office processes that can make you physically sick. Your annual performance review. Dreaded by managers because they have fifty pages of dorky questions to fill out about *each* of their 169 employees and dreaded by the rest of us because our review typically sucks. The annual performance review has become a much-hated American institution. I recently read that many American workers decide to take a sick day on the day of their review. Not a bad idea.

"THE CHEESE STANDS ALONE...
THE CHEESE STANDS ALONE..."

To begin with, there is the self-appraisal part that must be filled out, of course, by your SELF. I'll never forget the time I was stupid enough to answer the question "What do you think you need to improve upon?" Like a fool, I noted a few minor things. Sure enough, the my final performance review had the EXACT items I had cited, under the category, **Improvements Needed.**

Silly me. When I filled out the original form I thought my words were confidential. Only to be shared between me and my supervisor for purposes of professional development. Instead, my self-deprecating essay became a permanent fixture in the Great Files of the Human Resources department for the next millennium. If that company ever creates a time capsule for posterity you can be sure they will fill it with their HR papers including *my* darn self-evaluation form.

So, remember, when asked that bothersome question about what you need to do to improve your work skills, copy the following word for word: "**NOTHING. Absolutely nothing. I'm perfect. I know everything there is to know**."

Speaking of that enlightening performance review I am reminded of one I experienced two years later. I worked my butt off for a full twelve months at Company ABC. Played the game, dotted all my p's and q's, was a real Girl Scout. So, thinking it was time to reap what I had sowed, I gave myself an outstanding write-up on my self-evaluation form. Those motivational seminar facilitators would have been proud. Blow your own horn? I was blasting my accolades at 350 decibels. Wouldn't you know it? I still got a "C."

"I hope this doesn't dampen your enthusiasm, Amy," my boss called after me as I stomped my way out of his office. Maybe those postal workers have the right idea.

<u>How to Survive Corporate Office Processes and Keep What's Left of Your Dignity</u>

- Stock up on No-Doze™. You'll need it for corporate training films and it can also come in handy for those spontaneous department meetings that start at 5:00 PM.

- Hire a personal attorney, a personal assistant or a personal ANYTHING to help you understand all the paperwork you have to wade through and sign. Although it might be pricey, you'll save yourself hours of aggravation.

- Create a large opening in one of your file cabinets: label it *Bureaucracy.* Maybe you better make that two openings. Or four file cabinets.

- Keep copies of EVERYTHING you sign; you may actually want read the stuff some day. Or use it to help train that new puppy.

- Keep a humor book of some sort on your desk, especially for those days where Dysfunction Follows Form—office form that is.

Chapter 12: The Internet: The Information Stupor-Highway

One fine spring morning I was greeted by my friend, Will, in MIS. "Hi Amy, I hear you have a virus." "Shhhh, Will. Keep your voice down!" *I wash daily, take vitamins and practice safe sex. How could this happen?* "Uh, I mean your computer. I'm here to fix it for you."

Work in the nineties. You never know what will greet you first thing in the morning.

I use a computer every day of my life. When I get into the office, the third thing I do is turn on my PC. First, the purse goes in the drawer. Second, the lights come on. Next, I bring my trusty old computer to life. I have a love-hate relationship with it.

Whirring away next to me, some days my PC feels like a welcome substitute for my cat. Reassuring. Friendly. A bit awkward to hug but definitely appreciated.

Other days I'm ready to take a sledgehammer to it. Like the times I am trying to finish a project for the V.P. of Marketing and it dies. Or the times the constant noise of the machine gives me a headache and I turn it off for the day, hoping to just relax with good ole' paper and pen. Then the phone rings and my boss asks, "Did you get that important e-mail I sent you? Please check the attachment because I need some answers in six minutes." *Shoot! I have to turn on the darn machine AGAIN? Isn't the nine hours, 23 minutes and 11 seconds we just spent together enough?* Moments like that my computer tries my patience. Like a needy husband or a cranky child.

Then there's what appears on it. I am blessed with several acquaintances who like e-mail. They often receive funny—and not so funny—entries over the wires which they like to share. Lucky me.

One day these purportedly *real* headlines that were bestowed upon me by a colleague: *Chef Throws His Heart into Helping Feed Needy; War Dims Hope for Peace; Red Tape Holds Up New Bridges.* In addition to these valuable lessons: *One seventh of your life is spent on Mondays. Anything worth fighting for is worth fighting dirty for. Someone who thinks logically is a nice contrast to the real world. By the time you make ends meet, they move the ends.* Not to mention the e-mail transmissions I've received about The Magical Grapefruit of Love or the Top Twenty Reasons Why Chocolate is Better than Sex.

Over the past two years I have also been the recipient of great messages of paranoia via electronic mail. One day I got a piece which described a well-known database company that amassed vital information—name, address, social security number—on EVERYONE in the world and was selling it as part of their service package. Call me a skeptic but when I read this I wondered—EVERYONE? How did they collect this data on obscure tribes in South America or college students doing internships in the Arctic Circle?

Months later I received news about a pager that *automatically* sends personal information about its owner to various unknown and nasty people. All by itself? I can just see it at the box office now: *Return of the Killer Pagers.* I'll bet you'll never look at yours quite the same way again.

And for the first prize winner in the Pushing Paranoia Over the Electronic Airwaves contest, I mustn't forget this version of Santa Claus is Coming to Town:

You better watch out

You better not cry
You better not pout
I'm telling you why
Santa Claus is tapping your phone.

Charming. Not only do we have paranoid folks out there but evil ones as well.

One day over e-mail I received a four page document entitled 50 Ways to Confuse, Worry or Just Scare the Beejeezus Out of People in the Computer Lab. I think personal computers have created a new species: Bored, Psychotic *and* Sado-masochistic Human Beings. Who else would take the time to write this kind of stuff and post it?

Here are more of my favorites:

My buddy got busted for counterfeiting. He was making pennies. They caught him because he was putting the heads and tails on the wrong sides. He's in a minimum security prison now; he's on a whiffle-ball and chain.

I just got skylights put in my place. The people who live above me are furious.

I got food poisoning today. I don't know when I'm going to use it.

Am I the only one left who WORKS in the world? Then there are the flaming radicals who show up across my screen to brighten my day with such ditties: *Your action is necessary to thwart the attempts by the telephone companies to assess additional charges to our phone bills for access the Internet.*
I see. Some hacker nerd wants me to write a letter to the FCC to ask them to take a stance against the billion dollar telephone industry, just so she can continue to send literary masterpieces like this and the other messages around the world?

The Male Definition of a Successful Date:

Age 17 Tongue

Age 25 Breakfast

Age 35 She didn't set back my therapy

Age 48 I didn't have to meet her kids

Age 66 Got home alive

I don't think so.

My daily torture in the form of electronic mail letters does not stop with text files. There are graphic images, as well, designed to cause the average corporate employee to go mad in under 72 hours. Like pictures of partridges, geese, turtle doves, French hens and other forms of poultry created using only keyboard symbols. The techno-nerd's version of "The Twelve Days of

Christmas." Or the guardian angel and Star Trek characters also formed only from commas, periods, semi-colons and parentheses.

I'll never forget the time a friend sent me a cat icon for my computer system. Barely one-half inch long, gray, white and fluffy, this computer-generated kitty did everything real cats like to do. Drink milk, play with a ball of yarn, eat mice and, yes, even take a dump in the litter box. It was easy to install and looked cute zipping around my screen when I clicked on my mouse. For about three minutes. Non-stop.

As I attempted to do my work --- a novel concept for computer-use these days--- a little kitten would get in the way of my spreadsheet, my paragraph, my database entry...my EVERYTHING. Have you ever tried to tap out something important for your senior manager when an insipid little animal is peeing on your page?

???
KITTY SCREEN SAVER

On December 27, 1996 I read this headline in the Saint Paul *Pioneer Press*: AVERAGE AMERICAN EMPLOYEE WASTES FOUR AND ONE HALF HOURS A WEEK. Yeah. And I know on what. (By the way, shouldn't that say four and one half DAYS per week?)

The man who spouted this gem, Michael Dertouzos of the M.I.T. lab for Computer Science, should be knighted: "E-mail is an open duct into your central nervous system. It occupies the brain and reduces productivity."

Speaking of the horrors of e-mail, the Internet isn't much better. Every time I use it to search for information on a specific topic, I get a minimum of 1,629,551 hits. "Would you like to narrow your search?" the machine sweetly asks me as I feel an anxiety attack coming on because my findings are due in fifteen minutes. Would I like to take a crowbar to this machine right now?

Internet, Shminternet. Who needs it? Not workers, that's for sure. The last conversation I had about the Internet I learned you could find the following over it: *Best Hotels for Those Under Six or Over Eighty-Five in Martha's Vineyard; Great Deals on Discontinued Aquarium Decor; Seven New Swear Words in Polish and Their Translations; Easy Recipes for Freezer-Burned Beef Jerky; Everything You Wanted to Know about Christmas Tree*

Farms in Fiji. If you ask me, we should all go back to knitting and carving wood.

Membership Requirements for joining WHTI: (We Hate the Internet)

- A copy of the book *How to be Your Own Best Friend*; you'll need it after 98% of the human race drops you because they don't know how to use a telephone to say hello.

- Four to six months' personal experience shopping in empty malls; everyone else is doing it on the Internet.

- A mate that likes real hugs, not cyber ones.

- A list of The Top Ten Best Things About Reading Documents Made Out of Paper—if you can remember what they are.

- Storage space in your garage for old technology called television sets; you'll make a killing when society gets tired of watching stuff on their computer monitors and longs for the good old days.

Chapter 13: Amy in MeetingLand: What a Long, Strange Trip It's Been

It is a fact of life around Corporate America and always has been. It is often tedious, usually involves other people and sometimes includes food. No, it's not the company Christmas party. It's the all-hated, mostly-feared and rarely revered "M" word: Meeting. I have been to so many meetings during my years in Corporate America, it's a miracle I've gotten any work done.

In my speeches to professionals in transition I always ask the audience to compile a list of Most Hated Work Activities. On my list, MEETINGS is always Number One. Too bad you can't just tape record your thoughts on a particular work topic and submit it to some Meeting Master. The Meeting Master is like a one-man-band and takes care of the issue under discussion by all by herself. She sits in a small, dimly-lit conference room and listens to a half dozen tapes from meeting participants. She is the only one who suffers through the lengthy diatribes of her colleagues. For all her pain she earns the power to make all the decisions.

Participants are happy as well: No waiting for all parties to arrive in Conference Room X. No waiting for unpleasant pleasantries to be over with. No listening to other humans moan and groan with little action being taken. Hence, NO MEETING!

Over the years I have attended meetings to die for—almost literally. There was one session where twenty-five of us were asked to gather around the company's fanciest conference room to behold the New Guiding Light—a word processing program created by God and His angels, no doubt. The lights were dimmed as a large white screen was lowered in front of our hungry eyes. A faint drum roll could be heard from far off. Fireworks could be glimpsed out of the back window of the building. Clinging to the edge of our seats, we viewed page after page of the latest and greatest in fonts, pagination techniques and ways how to integrate documents with our firm's e-mail package. This software package was such a miracle—it would increase our inventory turns, enhance revenues and stabilize our R&D budget, all within 24 hours.

As I stopped to catch my breath and wipe a tear, I heard it. Subtle at first, but becoming louder with each passing moment.

Zzzzzzz. *Was there a fly in the room?* As I furtively glanced around the room my eyes fell upon the culprit. My colleague, John, was dozing in his chair right next to mine. At this company meeting where two boring people did all of the talking, the lights were down low, and not a cookie crumb was in sight, he had actually fallen asleep. Not a bad idea.

Meetings bring out the worst in people. Like the time I spilled an entire cup of water on my new silk blouse in the middle of an intense discussion about market strengths and weaknesses. Or the time a colleague decided to have an asthma attack while explaining the virtues of our next generation product.

I have also found that at meetings these personality types surface amongst the most otherwise normal people:

- The Snide Quipster: the person who adds little to the meeting except sarcastic spears he hurls at other speakers' ideas.
- The Moaner: the person who complains about everything but never offers a solution to a problem.
- Johnny-Come-Lately: the person who dashes into the room ten minutes late, spends the entire meeting updating his Day-Timer and leaves early for the next meeting he's late for.
- The Little Hitler: the person who dictates plans to everyone, never once asking for feedback.

- The Pollyanna: the person who agrees with everyone and has the backbone of a turtle made of cherry Jello™.

I'll never forget the meeting I facilitated for a group of middle managers. To liven things up I created handouts on bright blue paper, bought chocolate candy wrapped in shiny gold paper and decided to play a little game. It wasn't a game, really, but rather an innovative way to introduce people to each other. Each person was to state their name (not too difficult, theoretically), their function at the company (*if* they remembered it) and ONE thing you could not tell about them by their outward appearance. Easy right? Well, these eight adult human beings—who were rather nice people when you spoke with them individually—suddenly turned into *the* most dull, inexpressive slabs of meat you'd ever find stalking the cubicle walls. Not ONE of them could come up with an interesting, colorful or non-work oriented piece of information about themselves. No personal passions for motorcycle racing, chocolate mousse, or even their favorite color. I wasn't asking for deep, dark secrets, folks. We are just talking about a little bit of life-beyond-the-organization.

One guy I knew had just been on the front cover of a local sports magazine for his track record in rollerblading. Even *he* was speechless! Last time *I* try to bring levity into the world of meetings.

I also recall a meeting I attended that was supposed to bring people of similar rank together to get to know each other. After two hours of mundane presentations, a mundane buffet lunch was served. Everyone was encouraged to "mingle" and sit with people they didn't know very well. You have never seen groups of human beings from the *same* department laden with paper plates filled with potato salad and ham sandwiches, congregate so *quickly* around small conference-room tables. Accounting folks were in one corner, marketing people in the next and operations took up the middle. So much for inter-departmental bonding. My colleague, Fred, once told me about a meeting he was sentenced to attend.

The corporation he worked for at the time was trying to improve intra-departmental communications. They hired a consultant and rented a room in a local hotel. It was downhill from there. After a myriad of well-intentioned yet faltering question-and-answer sessions the consultant asked "Now, what tasks are you NOT doing at work that you should be? Who would like to be first?" Unbelievable. This guy expected people to pipe up and confess their sins among a group of sixty other colleagues *plus* their superiors.

...I WAS CAUGHT
PLAYING COMPUTER
SOLITAIRE AT WORK!
Elena '98

I can just see it now: "Well instead of writing that monthly status report I've been playing Solitaire on my computer." "Uh, you know that software bug I was supposed to fix last week? I decided to surf the Net for a new snowboard instead. Sorry." Yet another case of the "M" word blues strikes in Corporate America.

We can't forget the IMFH--Interminable Meeting From Hell. You've heard of the Terminator Man? The Interminable Meeting is far more dangerous. Here are the telling signs: Lack of air in a hermetically sealed conference room. Several colleagues speaking monotonously about a topic misunderstood by the majority of attendees. Nothing for sustenance but a cold cup of coffee. Not to worry, however. The only repercussions of attending the IMFH are that it will render you lifeless, brain-dead, confused and begging for mercy within a matter of two hours. Tests have proven that complete recovery is rare but a week-long vacation in Hawaii might be a good start.

Five Suggestions For Office Meeting Survival in Corporate America:

- Bribe, cajole and coerce all attendees into agreeing to let you run the show. Create and stick to a five minute agenda.

- Bring an egg timer and place it in the middle of the table. Set it to 10 minutes. When the thing goes off, stand up and leave the room. Conversation will probably continue as if nothing happened and you can take credit for having attended the meeting.

- Encourage others to hold meetings at the local public park, around the volleyball net. That way when you don't get anything done at least you've had a good workout and don't have to go to the gym that night.

- Bring in your favorite compact discs and audio tapes. Explain to your colleagues that you can only concentrate with music playing.

- Explain to participants they can only attend the meeting if they have the right password. Forget to tell anyone the password—other than yourself.

Chapter 14: Communication is the Key: Too Bad Someone Threw it in the Trash

People pay millions of dollars each year to attend seminars on it. Audio tapes and books are published every forty seconds on it. Community college classes, radio and television shows, newspapers and magazines are always talking about it. Sex, right? Wrong!

Communication. Defined by *Webster's* as, "the act of transmitting; a giving or exchanging of information, signals, or messages by talk, gestures, writing, etc." Communication in the office is *not* a many-splendor thing. Although good communication is crucial to the success of any business enterprise, we have managed to survive and even prosper without it in this country. The forms communication takes within our hallowed walls of commerce can vary greatly. There is an entire caste system of communication techniques at the office.

For example: One morning I got a phone call from a sales rep who was trying desperately to sell me her product. I reviewed it one month earlier and was quite impressed. "Did you do it?" Rhonda the Rep asks in a hushed tone over the telephone.
"Do what?" I responded, raising my voice ever so slightly in the hopes she'll do the same. "You know, the memo." "Memo? Won't an e-mail do, Rhonda?" I grumbled as I quickly remembered the promise I made to her to write a memo to my boss, recommending we buy her product. I resented being called on my error at 8:30 in the morning, before I've had my second cup of herbal tea. (In fact, it's people like Rhonda that *force* me into needing a second cup of herbal tea.) "Amy, you told me when I was in your office last week that you were going to write a hard copy memo to your boss about our product! DON'T YOU REMEMBER? Not just an e-mail message but an actual MEMORANDUM!" Oh well. I guess I should have done the memo.

In the corporate arena e-mail packs less of a punch than a real-honest-to-goodness-8 by 10 inch-white-bond-paper memorandum. You can hold it in your hand, you can set it on fire, you can sit on it and fly it around the office in the form of a little airplane. Thus, a hard copy memo can do a lot that e-mail cannot.

At the same time, however, e-mail is extremely effective for those quick and dirty—well, I guess they can't be too dirty, that's against the law—messages exchanged between office personnel. It's great for those touchy subjects that used to be handled by mature adults talking face to face. For example:

"Uh, boss, can I have a raise?"

"NO!"

See? Because you had this dialogue online it was fast, to the point and you didn't have to look the jerk in the eye. In spite of the joys of computer-based communication, the old-fashioned concept of exchanging ideas still lingers in some of offices around the country. You may have heard of it. It's called "talking." You know, when two human beings express thoughts and feelings via verbal discourse using mouths and/or hand gestures.

Unfortunately, those of us in very high tech offices still have to resort to this outdated mode of conveying information when—God forbid—the computer network goes down. The last time that happened at my office, everyone was walking around the building, humming, with a glazed look in their eyes. They were trying to remember what forming words felt like.

"WHAT SHE IS SAYING..."

"WHAT THE CUSTOMER HEARS..."

Talking too, however, can be precarious. I'll never forget one incident that haunted me for months. I was asked by one of our sales executives the cost of acquiring an extra product manual for his customer. Since I worked in the marketing department at the time I knew the person who was responsible for writing the manuals and placed a call to her office. That was my first mistake. Over the phone, I heard him say "$8500." *Pricey,* I thought, but I knew our products were expensive and the manual was in a non-paper form called CD ROM (yet another member of the office communications caste system). I therefore did not question this price and simply reported it to the salesperson who passed it along to his anxious customer. What a mess *that* turned out to be! The customer thought the price was outrageous and went out of control. He expressed his dismay to the sales rep who then wrote me a rather hostile "ARE YOU SURE ABOUT THAT PRICE?" e-mail message the next morning. After much ado I determined that my colleague in the manual-making department had quoted me the amount of "85 to 100 dollars," ***not*** eighty-five-hundred-dollars!! Serves me right for trying to communicate via human speech.

That whole nightmare reminds me of a training film about communication I saw in a junior high English class. A conservative-looking man received twelve neatly pressed white skirts rather than the dozen white *shirts* he ordered, due to—you guessed it—poor communication. Junior high school, the office, the grocery store—we experience it everywhere.

But the thing that kills me is that most folks don't take responsibility for their information-exchange foul-ups. I have a dear friend that is an Executive Assistant at a large manufacturing company. While we were having a brief telephone chat, one August afternoon, she was interrupted four times by a member of her department. The member was supposed to meet some people for lunch that day and didn't remember the name of the restaurant. This guy was in much distress. As my friend, the Assistant, tried to straighten things out for the starving executive I couldn't help but laugh. Did that guy ever think of calling his lunch partners directly —via cell phone? Or how about calling the restaurant after my friend relayed the name of it to him the ***first time***? Maybe what we all need is the latest and greatest from Miracle Ear.™ But my suggestions may suffice.

Five Ways to Improve Human to Human Communication At the Office:

- Hand out a set of flashcards with key office phrases to everyone who works there.

- Get the health care providers to offer free prescription glasses, contact lenses, hearing aids, sign language classes, lapel microphones---whatever it takes.

- Send all employees to an English as a First Language class.

- Hire the guy from *My Fair Lady* to give free diction and enunciation instruction.

- Limit all computer use to three days per week. That will *force* employees to talk or write notes to get their message across the other two days.

Chapter 15: Corporate Food Fest: How I Ruined My Eating Habits in Less Than 90 Days

I am a very special person. There are only five others like me in the United States. We are brave, indifferent to opposition. We are creative, pioneering people with little regard for public opinion. We are Those That Eat Out of Corporate Vending Machines. I'll tell you another shocker. I've been doing it for years. First of all, I like to eat. Second of all, I *need* to eat. Thirdly— I work in Corporate America, so who has time to cook?

One guy I work with makes me eat my heart out. (No pun intended.) Every day at approximately twelve noon he pulls out his Three Plastic Bags. One has a good-looking sandwich of some sort. Another caresses some loose-fitting munchie morsels like chips or pretzels. The third holds a piece of succulent, fresh-looking fruit. As I pass his cubicle, my shrink-wrapped two-day old, mushy, moldy machine-bought tuna salad sandwich in hand, I want to weep. I need a wife to pack *my* lunches! The last time I had a homemade, tasty sandwich for lunch was Memorial Day 1979. And *I* made it.

I do get some relief, however. Every once in a while there is a BIG MEETING going on in the building somewhere. You know, the kind that requires a catered lunch. If I'm lucky that day I hear the whispers between the cubicle walls.

"Did ya hear?"

"No, what?"

"There's FOOD at coffee station five."

That's when I'm blessed with a picked-over sweet roll, slice of dried-up veggie pizza or, if I'm real lucky, a leftover turkey on wheat with just the right amount of mayo. On those days, life is good.

There are other breaks from the Almighty Vending Machine. Food I actually bring from home. Alright, it's not Real Food, like the stuff my buddy munches on every day, but it is made up of particles that can be safely injested by humans. This stuff may be low in nutrients, but man, it's high on bulk.

FREE FOOD...
COFFEE STATION
FIVE!!

The problem is that now, when I think of mealtime I think of little boxes. Not the ticky-tacky kind that someone wrote a song about years ago to describe Daly City, California but literally, little boxes. Little cups and little cans, too. That's what many of my daily foodstuffs come in. If I didn't know better, I'd think I was training to be an astronaut.

It hasn't been an easy journey in the Galaxy of Gastronomic Investigations. First I tried those little cups of soup. Peel back the paper cover on the cup, add hot water and GO! A quasi-meal in just a few minutes. Alright, so the cups are short on quantity but I fixed that. I ate two. They are also long on salt. After months of slurping those critters I found myself drinking 25 cups of water a day, even on weekends. Apparently the damage had been done so I moved on.

Rather than sticking with the hot-water-to-bring-your-food-alive theme, I decided to get bold. I asked my husband to pick up those little cans of tuna fish packaged with everything you need to make tuna salad. Clean and neat. Portable and easy to assemble. Perfect for an anal retentive like me. Besides, I was a Girl Scout for many years. Tuna salad made with pickle relish and mayonnaise was a favorite of mine on camping trips. I'm an old pro at this.

You may not know this but tuna salad on crackers every day can get old.

Okay. Now I'll confess my *real* problem with the tuna-in-a-kit idea. Since my daily breakfast—an apple—rarely satisfies me, by 10:00 AM I ate the entire tuna ensemble and had fish breath to boot. I know. Self control, or more apples, was the logical solution. Rather than try either one of those, however, I moved on again. I just knew that with a little patience and some faith I would find the *perfect* pre-packaged lunch alternative to my vending machine delectables.

I next tried mashed-potatoes-in-a-cup. Kind of like the soup but this time potatoes. This plan was going along fine. I tried all the different flavors and it was fun. Garlic and Herbs. Sour Cream and onion. Chives and onion. Onion and Onion. Best of all I felt I was *finally* getting some kind of hearty meal, that was tasty AND easy to prepare at work. Then it happened.
One day I was doing my daily ritual at the hot water spigot. I guess I became distracted because, before I knew it, the contents of my Garlic and Herbs delight was strewn all over the purple Formica counter in the nearby coffee area.

My 20-year-old assistant, who happened to be standing next to me, grabbed my arm in horror and we simultaneously screamed, "Are you alright?!" After determining that, indeed, we had both survived the flight of the wayward cup, it was time for the dirty work. Everywhere I looked there were limp, half congealed potato bits marked with assorted colors including brown, green, red and yellow. The stuff seemed to spread in a menacing way—kind of like a liquid version of the protagonist in *The Blob*. To make matters worse, the proportions of water, dry potato buds, slimy ones and brightly colored spices oozing over the counter made the whole concoction look a whole lot like—you guessed it—VOMIT! The three of us immediately noticed this distressing similarity. While I kept silent, feeling already The Fool, my two comrades were not that subtle. They began cracking jokes to each other about the vile appearance of the slime and, finally, my assistant announced in a loud, clear voice, "This is why I'm not having children!" I couldn't help but crack a smile while the three of us continued feverishly to destroy the evidence and get the area ready again for public usage. After that day my beloved mashed potato cups have never quite been the same.

<u>How to Eat Lunch in Corporate America</u>

- Take a course in Survivalist training. Keep all the free samples they give you for your lunch box.

- Invest heavily in Kraft General Foods, Inc. They make a large amount of products that come in small plastic cups that can be easily consumed. Perfect for the corporate employee.

- Sabotage your company's computer network at least once a month. When the network goes down, you'll be forced to go out to lunch. Better yet, the MIS department might cater something for everyone since they feel so guilty.

- With part of your annual bonus, hire a nurturing grandmotherly type to come to your house every day for a month, at 7:00 AM, to make your lunch. While she's there, have her fix you breakfast, too. Get as much bang for your buck as you can.

- Quit your job and find a new one—three blocks from home. Lunch hours will never be the same.

Chapter 16: Revenge of the Gizmos: Office Machinery and Electronics

I thought it was a simple request. Silly me. For weeks I asked for access to a printer that was somewhat near my cube, rather than trekking the two miles to the other side of the building every time I needed to pick up my work. And once I got there, I had to fight my way through the masses of people and paper to find my documents. It was worse than Moscow's bread lines.

One day my prayers paid off—or so I thought. The MIS rep grinned broadly as she wheeled a fairly weathered, but still functional, laser printer right outside my cubicle wall. *WOW! This could be heaven. No more long hikes to get my stuff out of the printer. I could roll my chair over to the darn machine without even having to get up.* After the installation hoopla subsided, I swung into action. I finished writing the memo that showed on my monitor and pressed "OK" in the print dialog box. Rubbing my hands together in glee, I felt like a new woman. No more fighting for printer time. No more time consuming hikes across the office, no more.... *What was that AWFUL noise?* As I got up to investigate the source of that annoying SCREECH-CLUNK-SPIT, SCREECH-CLUNK-SPIT to my horror, I realized I didn't have much searching to do. The culprit lay right outside my cubicle wall. After twenty minutes of 'enjoying' my new printer I was ready for either a job transfer or admission to the local loony bin. Every filling in my mouth was ringing and the hairs on my neck were doing an about-face. What do they say? Be careful what you ask for?

And speaking of printers, do you remember the scene in one of the *I Love Lucy* television shows when Lucille Ball is making rice? Well, that was me one day when I got a hold of an overzealous printer. For every page I asked it to print, it spit out five. Then, when I thought the end of the file had finally been reached, the thing kept going and going and going. Luckily, a friendly colleague stopped by and was coerced into helping me clean up the mess. We stuffed five recycling bins with the wayward sheets of 8 ½" by 11" paper and had to step outside for a cold drink. All I can say is beware of Possessed Printers from Purgatory.

Then there was the copier from hell. Now, I've used many a copying machine in my time. I have been Behind the Lettered

Door enough where I could open doors A through E in less than twenty seconds. I've replaced toner cartridges of all shapes and sizes—and only ruined two blouses—and braved hot metal bars to liberate dozens of innocently jammed pieces of paper. But this machine really called my bluff. Every other day when I ventured over to make my unassuming stack of two or three single-sided standard-sized copies, it had a different message for me:

"Error 2333—lift cover, clear glass, check door Z."

"Toner low, paper jammed, error code unknown."

"Account F114; check manual and clear drawer C."

It must had have a vendetta against me because the thing was relentless. After fighting hundreds of battles with it, I finally caved in. Gave up. Threw in the towel. The Office Services lady—the one who has the copier repairperson's phone number—has become my best friend. I now have an account at the local florist and keep stacks of boxed candy in my desk. Believe me, it's worth it.

I'll also never forget the violent scene I witnessed one day in the copier-printer-fax room at work. One of our newest secretaries, typically a sweet, quiet woman, was screaming at the top of her lungs at the fax machine. "I'm going to kill you! I'm going to take a machete to you if you don't start working, darnit!" Pollyanna turned into the Wicked Witch in just a few short minutes. Office machines can do that to you. I should probably note here

STOP!!
Elena '98

that I had great empathy for my co-worker. The very same fax machine that was being threatened that afternoon also had it in for me. Every time I would quietly saunter up to the gray molded-plastic terror the green light came on. It was as if I had some magnetic device pinned to my belly button. The closer I got, the quicker the light turned on, signaling an *incoming* fax. Then the green light was always followed by those horrible three words that every office worker loves to hate "COMMUNICATING, PLEASE WAIT." Faxing is now the "F" word in my book.

Then there was the safety light incident. One morning I was sitting in my trusty old 2' by 4'—cubicle that is—minding my own business. All of the sudden the lights went out. My PC went dead and the whole place went silent for just a second. Then the complaining started.

"Darn it! I just finished typing five pages and didn't have a chance to save the file!"

"Is this another stupid Emergency Drill?"

"Do they have to do this right before lunch? I'm hungry!" Colleagues in funny red hats started racing around the cubicles explaining to everyone there had been a power outage in our block and that everyone should exit the building immediately. Thank God they had flashlights with them because our entire corridor was pitch black. Wouldn't you know it? The safety lights, which ran on batteries and were supposed to be our saving grace during these times of trial and tribulation, were, well, missing. I mean, for some reason or other they *did not exist.*

Two days later I was gifted with an emergency light that could have lit up Times Square in the middle of a snowstorm. It plugged directly into an electrical outlet under my desk and stayed on ALL THE TIME. By the time we moved to a new building months later, I looked like I'd been sitting on the beach in Maui for several weeks, without a drop of sunscreen. Whoever said that work and play don't mix?

<u>How to Coexist With Office Electronics</u>

- Keep a custom-fit set of Knights of the Roundtable armor stashed in your desk drawer for when those machines decide to act up. Also works as a great costume for the company contest on Halloween.

- Suggest an extra tourniquet for the office first aid kit. Comes in handy for wrapping up and hauling out uncooperative office machines.

- Keep an extra hammer or wrench in the drawer next to the coffee machine. Much more effective than swift kicks to the copier or pounding of fists on other non-functional company assets.

- Invest in a very old laptop computer, automobile sized fax machine and cellular phone. If you're away from the office, what you don't use can't annoy you. If these portable mobile machines give you a hard time, just toss them.

- Take a class in American history. Figure out how we used to process paperwork back in the old days. If we ever decide to ban all office machines, you're ahead of the game.

Chapter 17:
Getting Back Home (to Myself): Confessions of A Corporate Warrior

Standing in the foyer of an upscale Bay Area restaurant with new my brother-in-law, while our spouses were in the bathrooms, I was *almost* at a loss for words—which is rare for me! Jeff had just been laid off from a large pharmaceutical company after only eight months. My husband and my sister also had their work challenges to deal with.

"So, you're the only one of the four of us who doesn't have some kind of tumult in your life," he said with a questioning look in his eyes.

"Yes, that's right. I feel very blessed at this time in my life. Things are going well." Little did he know what it took to get there! I then went on to explain, in a condensed manner so I wouldn't put the poor guy to sleep, that it wasn't always like this for me. I hinted that there was a time I was in between corporate jobs for two and a half years. As he started to turn a pale shade of green, I realized it wasn't the best thing to mention to a newly released corporate warrior. After hugging my sister and her husband good-bye, I remained deep in thought.

There are so many Jeffs and Bobs and Denises and Barbaras out there, being 'let go' seems to be the norm these days. The few folks on the planet who have *never* had the corporate ax fall are walking around, slightly paranoid. They're not alone.

The other day my boss called me in to tell me "something." As she began talking I was rewriting my resume in my mind. (As it turned out she simply wanted to tell me about a department reorganization.)

I also have my moments when, after a bad day at the work, I think, *Oh Well. At least I can type! Heck, I can even wait on tables!* Do you know how much those wait-persons in fancy restaurants earn in tips on a good night?

The point is, it never stops. When you're out of work (and you're not yet a self-appointed entrepreneur, independently wealthy, or have won the lottery) you're nervous and depressed because you desperately want to *belong.* To a corporation.

Then when you're *there*, in the end-all-be-all J-O-B, you walk around with your head tipped slightly to one side, trying to see what's coming up from behind that could knock you off your guard. You're *still* nervous. Perhaps moreso than before. What to do? What to do?

Start your own company, you say? Maybe. But self-employment isn't for everyone. I'll never forget a community college professor I recently had who described a test that any aspiring business owner could take to determine if she/he was entrepreneur material. Listening to the teacher, I felt stunned and these thoughts whirled through my head: *Well, I had my own business for a while and, yeah, I didn't really make a lot of money, but, well, it was during the recession and, and...you fool! Why didn't you just take that darn test and save yourself a lot of trouble!* There is a certain personality type that fits beautifully into the Entrepreneur's New Clothes. I guess I wore the wrong size at the time.

Others of us seem to do better working for The Man (or Woman). If that's you then here is one take-it-or-leave-it word of wisdom: COMPARTMENTALIZE. Consider your job as a life 'project'. One that takes more time than the others, that's all.

We humans are multi-faceted and so are our lives. Work is only one part of our patchwork quilt of activity and should be treated as such. Let's not give it more attention than necessary. Please.

Granted, work is our source of livelihood, but, if you have already manifested a few corporate jobs in your life, I'll bet you have some friends or family members that will help feed and shelter you if it ever gets *that bad.* You know what I mean. Even CEOs of large companies, who spend many hours at the office have families, friends and hobbies. If they *don't,* then at least they have to spend *some* time going to the bathroom or getting a hair cut! They can't fool me. Bottom line? A job isn't EVERYTHING.

I have never heard of a human being who has died because they were laid off from a corporate job. In fact, I recently read a tragic tale of a young Japanese man who committed suicide because he had too *much* work.

When I was teenager I remember hearing of an accomplished stockbroker who dropped dead of a heart attack at his own retirement party. I don't think his behavior was in response to the gold watch he received as a gift. Unless, of course, it was purchased at a discount store and he was expecting something from Cartier. I guess we'll never know.